ENGLAND AND
THE OCTOPUS

BY THE SAME AUTHOR IN
COLLABORATION WITH
A. WILLIAMS-ELLIS

THE PLEASURES OF ARCHITECTURE

Reproduced by permission of the Proprietors of "Punch."]

1914. Mr. William Smith answers the Call to preserve his Native Soil Inviolate.

1919. Mr. William Smith comes back again to see how well he has done it.

ENGLAND AND THE OCTOPUS

By
CLOUGH
WILLIAMS-ELLIS

WITH A NEW FOREWORD BY
JONATHAN DIMBLEBY
PRESIDENT OF CPRE
AND AN EPILOGUE BY
PATRICK ABERCROMBIE
*Professor of Town Planning at
Liverpool University*

Geoffrey Bles   Suffolk St., Pall Mall
London

FIRST PUBLISHED 1928
THIS EDITION PUBLISHED 1996 BY CPRE
BY KIND PERMISSION OF THE PORTMEIRION ESTATE

This facsimile edition of ENGLAND AND THE OCTOPUS has been sponsored and produced by The Beacon Press as a contribution to CPRE's 70th anniversary celebration and to show our concern for the environment. Beacon operates an environmental management system approved under British Standard 7750 and the EC Eco-Management and Audit Scheme.

1996 FOREWORD

THIS IS A POLEMICAL BOOK, WRITTEN BY A SPIRITED and angry young man. In 1929, Clough Williams-Ellis was not the household name he was to become, but his views were formed and he had a clear sense of mission. In *England and the Octopus* he waged war on ugliness, thoughtlessness, selfishness and short-sightedness, detailing the catastrophic consequences of these human frailties on the precious quality of rural England. In so doing, he - in effect - set out an uncompromising credo for CPRE, which was then in its infancy.

The 'octopus' in question was London, but could have been any English metropolis, its tentacles stretching out, apparently unstoppably, into a countryside that was fast losing its integrity and identity. Unconstrained by today's niceties, Williams-Ellis uses refreshingly robust language to denounce the 'spate of mean building ... that is shrivelling up the old England'; to castigate its perpetrators: 'What vindictive monsters must their builders be - what a grudge they must have against England and against generations of Englishmen yet unborn!', and to immortalise those without sensibility and sensitivity to the quality of their surroundings as the 'unburied dead'.

The book is worth reprinting for the author's 'Devil's Dictionary' alone. His tirade against advertisement hoardings, broadcasting masts, golf courses and petrol pumps is a reminder of how, in some respects, the battlefield is unchanged. At the same time, it is impossible to read this book without recognising that in the generations since it was published, we have done far more damage - with the car, our appetite for material goods and the great urban exodus - than even Clough Williams-Ellis had imagined.

But this is neither a gloomy nor a nostalgic book. The author has faith. He believes that if we open our eyes we shall see what needs to be done. His passionate advocacy of quality and sensitivity in design, his insistence that standardisation can be avoided, and his belief that we can do better in the future than we have in the past combine realism with hope.

'Let us try to believe that some day, in spite of all, our descendants will be aware of beauty and amenity and will so live that loveliness is increased in their land because of them, and

1996 Foreword

shall be no longer despised and trampled underfoot.' Those are the words of Clough Williams-Ellis but they could have been written by anyone who cherishes rural England and is committed to the cause of its protection.

JONATHAN DIMBLEBY

President, CPRE
December 1996.

FOREWORD

There is nothing weighty or authoritative about the gadfly, yet for all that its sting has sometimes so tickled or exasperated the noblest of the brutes that his plunging reactions have changed the very course of history.

The generously endowed English seem to have been given a special immunity against visual beauty that only the most violent attacks can break through, and it is in the hope of piercing the thick and often calloused skins of my countrymen, and injecting a little doubt and discomfort, that I have deliberately envenomed my small dart.

Individuals as well as classes can well defend themselves, and I am less concerned about being wholly just to them than in shocking them into some realisation of what their defenceless England is becoming through the acts and omissions of its prodigal people as a whole.

The biological use and justification of pain is to give warning of damage or ill-health, and the following pages are designed to provoke a sensibility that must mean discomfort for the reader rather than pleasure. A state of things that some of us already find intolerable can only be changed

Foreword

by enlisting, through pain, a great body of active sympathisers who have come to see that to go as you please is not always to arrive at what is pleasant.

C. W.-E.

Portmeirion
  March 1928.

CONTENTS

CHAP.		PAGE
1.	THE PRODIGAL PLANET	11
2.	WATCHMEN AND THIEVES	17
3.	OUR SHORT-SIGHTED FOREBEARS AND OUR FUTILE SELVES	24
4.	SOME CAUSES OF URBAN BEASTLINESS, AND OF THE CONSEQUENT RUSH TO ESCAPE	31
5.	NEW TOWNS FOR OLD	42
6.	THE TRAGIC FOLLY OF CASTLE MALORY	49
7.	THE ARCHFIEND AND THE ARCHANGEL	60
8.	DONKEYS, DRONES AND OSTRICHES	70
9.	THE GREAT HOUSE: ITS CONSERVATION AND CONVERSION	80
10.	THE BENEFICENT BUSYBODIES	91
11.	PROPAGANDA, POLITICS AND PRESS	106
12.	SURSUM CORDA	117
	A DEVIL'S DICTIONARY	125
	EPILOGUE	180

CHAPTER I

THE PRODIGAL PLANET

FOR 25,000 YEARS, MORE OR LESS, MAN OR near-man has inhabited this world of ours. Only for the last few thousand years do we know very much about him. Only for the past century or so has he given cause for alarm and despondency in his maltreatment of the earth's surface.

In all probability (so the authorities inform us) another 25,000,000 years or so will be lived through by humanity on this planet. If there is even the roughest sort of truth in these figures, the human race is after all very, very young, and may still be allowed a good deal of folly.

Certainly the thought of those millions of years ahead of us is somehow comforting—it does seem to give time in which to straighten out our muddles and mistakes, though it provides no good reason for our going on making them. Indeed, if we could count fairly confidently on the world coming to an end quite soon, that would be the only excuse for letting things slide—

the only excuse for not trying to tidy up and reform.

But we are, it seems, at the beginning of our lease, not the end of it—a long lease from Nature, who, though a kind landlord enough, is slow to repair the damage done by her vandal tenants.

For generations at least, the bed we make our children must lie in; and it is small comfort to those tenants who are civilised to be told that in geological time the present age of stupid exploitation is but as the twinkling of an eye. It has already lasted several generations—one of them ours—and its traces cannot pass away for many more as yet unborn.

Surely as human beings we ought to demand an ordered, reasonable, humanistic setting for our lives and an end to this planless scramble that would scarcely do credit to the lower animals.

In this matter we seem to have run suddenly backwards, or at least to have skidded dangerously from the neat and seemly ways of our great- or great-great-grandfathers. They had a general sense of order and beauty, and realised that appearances were not " mere " but had profound if subconscious reactions on the lives to which they were the background. Or if they did not realise it, they acted as though they did, leaving us towns and villages and an English countryside that have, alas! already become almost as legendary as some lovely fairy tale.

In many ways, perhaps in most, the charm of

the past is largely fictitious; but in grouped architecture and visual country amenity we have evidence enough to show how calamitously we have fallen below all other ages whatever in the very things that distinguish the civilised from the savage.

Can we bear to believe that we, the English people, have thus fallen from grace for ever, that never again will England be an island of unsmirched country and ordered towns? Let us rather try to believe that some day, in spite of all, our descendants will be aware of beauty and amenity, and will so live that loveliness is increased in their land because of them, and shall be no longer despised and trampled underfoot.

It is for that generation, perhaps remote, that we ourselves must hope and work. For it we must preserve what may be of our ancient heritage, for it proclaim the gospel of beauty in the common setting of our daily life, that desolation be stayed, that standards of graciousness may here and there persist or be set up as rallying points, from which order and beauty may set out to overcome and reclaim the wilderness.

The philosophical may object that the distempers of the time of which the following pages treat are no more than one symptom of a general *malaise*, by no means confined to those more visible aspects that have engaged the author's particular attention. The same critics will likewise complain that the remedies offered are no more than palliatives that cannot remove the root causes of the trouble, even if they should serve to alleviate certain immediate distresses.

Both objections are very just.

As, however, there seems to be no immediate prospect of fundamental changes in those wider spheres in which are expressed the philosophical and political genius of a people—changes that would go to the very seat of the disorders of the body politic—ameliorative measures are all that meanwhile seem possible in this as in other departments of our national life. These measures are here suggested in no great hope of even a gradual cure being thereby assisted, but rather because, if the major operation that is really necessary cannot be performed, it is perhaps better to try ointments and lotions than to do nothing at all. They may give local and temporary relief, and are in any case a refuge against despair.

Some of our self-inflicted wounds and sores are in their very nature incurable and will leave indelible scars upon this physical world of ours that will outlast humanity itself. Others will remain as blemishes for generations, perhaps for centuries; and if we can do even a little in the way of preventing that which is so abidingly disfiguring, so uncertain of cure, it would seem worth while, like the holding of a beleaguered city in the hope that something may survive to reward the rescuing host.

It is only a somewhat wilful faith in the ultimate sanity of the English people that can hearten one sufficiently to engage in a cause so seemingly lost. The relieving force is not yet even enrolled, let alone disciplined, and we have no proof that its steadiness or *morale* will be adequate to the enormous tasks that await it, to which each year, each day, we meanwhile add and add.

Everyone who reads this book—indeed, everyone who reads at all or has eyes in his head—knows that England has changed violently and enormously within the last few decades. Since the War, indeed, it has been changing with an acceleration that is catastrophic, thoroughly frightening the thoughtful amongst us, and making them sadly wonder whether anything recognisable of our lovely England will be left for our children's children.

Little enough will be left for our own latter days : already we begin to tell each other guardedly and secretly of remote places where things are still as they used to be, where brutal exploitation is not yet, and where there is no new building, or where such buildings as there may be are well-mannered and harmonious.

For—need it be said ?—it is chiefly the spate of mean building all over the country that is shrivelling up the old England—mean and perky little houses that surely none but mean and perky little souls should inhabit with satisfaction.

Yet for the sake of our countrymen and our good opinion of them we must hope and believe that the unfortunates who dwell therein are thoroughly miserable, furtive and ashamed, and by no means the creatures that would seem the only appropriate tenants of what the twentieth century has offered them as homes.

But what vindictive monsters must their builders be—what a grudge they must have against England and against generations of Englishmen yet unborn!

All of which, of course, is no more than oratorical nonsense.

We know well enough that decent, God-fearing, God-damning Englishmen live very contentedly in the pink asbestos bungalows; and if they chance to be on Salisbury Plain or Dartmoor or the South Downs, or some commanding hill in the Cotswolds or the Chilterns where they can be seen from miles around, they are the more content and very far from ashamed.

And the builders, even the speculative builders—they are charming. Most of them take a pride in their work, many of them are honest; and to be a builder or contractor at all bespeaks considerable enterprise and organising ability—qualities very valuable in the citizen.

And yet . . .

Here we have two parties, each estimable and perhaps without reproach in everything else, conspiring together to commit an outrage upon the mother that bore them.

We have become tender in these days; yet because these people are blind, and ignorant of what they do, are we to hold them guiltless? And who shall decide what is and what is not an outrage?

CHAPTER 2

WATCHMEN AND THIEVES

THERE BEING NO OFFICIAL GUARDIAN OF OUR country's beauty, its guardianship is by default in commission amongst the few who care for it; and it is generally and rightly held that in such matters those who care the most are therefore those who know. That, at any rate, is all the claim that can be made for the authority of the Amenity Protectionists: they have no formal charter, no credentials of infallibility, and they have no legal or executive power or say whatever. They are small though passionate voices crying in the wilderness, and no one need heed them or pay the smallest attention.

Nor, to be sure, do they—as yet. Being an almost (but not quite) negligible minority, they are prudently regarded as cranks—cranks too detached from the driving-shaft of the modern world to grip it effectively or to promote or retard its revolutions.

That, unfortunately, has some truth in it—or

has had; but various organisations, of which the Council for the Preservation of Rural England is typical, have recently been tightening things up, and it seems that power may yet be transmitted through these cranks—combined and ordered so as to deliver a synchronised and quite appreciable thrust, not only on public opinion, but also upon Parliament, and so ultimately altering the very laws of the land.

The horse having been well and truly stolen, we are about to stage the great national ceremony of locking the stable door—not quite fruitlessly, as we are fallen so low that even the remaining straw and the halter have become precious to us as emblems of our former wealth.

Having already had the larger part of the South Downs filched from us, together with the margins of the New Forest and most of our accessible seaboard (to say nothing of the Home Counties and, at an earlier date, our commons throughout the land), our proposed door-locking comes none too soon.

But can we lock the door effectively even on what is left us—are the would-be janitors strong enough and numerous enough to prevail against the horse-thieves? That is a very urgent question, and one that only the event will answer.

Still, as has been said, all those who really concern themselves with beauty or care about amenity are agreed that England is being rapidly disfigured, and we may accept this as a fact. To many, indeed, it seems the most humiliating and tragic fact of the twentieth century. Cultivated people of all classes must deplore what is happening; the unseeing and unthinking (also of all classes) are no doubt more or less indifferent; but there can surely be none so perverted as actually to welcome and applaud this mass violation. Pure and whole-hearted diabolists are as rare in æsthetics as in morals, but that there are those who will still or defy their consciences for the sake of personal gain—in any place and at any time—is incontestable. We are probably all ready to sin against the light to *some* extent (if we are well enough rewarded); and our consciences are as individual and personal as the palms of our hands.

A.'s quasi-religious zeal about the sacredness of natural beauty and our duty towards it in right building may seem as queer and wrong-headed to his neighbour B. as B.'s perturbation over blasphemy or sexual unconventionality may seem to A. Yet B.'s sort have all the might, majesty and power of the law and the Churches on their side.

You may ravish and defile the most divine landscape in the world, and your children (being your children) will rise up and call you progressive. You are a " lucky prospector " or a " successful real-estate operator," a " live wire " and what local newspapers call " a prominent and respected citizen." By your exploitation of the land you have enriched yourself and your heirs. You have done very well.

God's footstool! How convenient for the unscrupulous to sharpen their claws upon! How tattered is it becoming, how for ever gone and forgotten its first fresh comeliness!

If we technically blaspheme—mere perishable words—we are threatened with hell-fire *and/or* six months' hard labour. For a hastily expressed thought we incur not merely odium, but penalties, definite and severe.

Yet for a deliberate act, brutally disregardful of natural beauty, essentially anti-social, sacrilegious and blasphemous, we receive the protection of the State, the accommodation of the banks, the approbation of our fellows, and the toleration of the Churches.

In the late War we were invited to fight to preserve England. We believed, we fought. It may be well to preserve England, but better to have an England worth preserving. We saved our country that we might ourselves destroy it.

Possibly that is the only road to pacifism—to destroy all that is fair and of good repute in our own country, all that fosters our pride and our love, so that we shall no longer care greatly what becomes of it, nor show any feeling save surprise should a foreign invader think it worth appropriating.

Certainly the dangerous adventure of war, even the probability of death or mutilation, offered a more attractive prospect to many of our countrymen than did their normal life in England.

" The response of the Black Country and

the industrial North has been magnificent—the patriotism of these simple, toil-worn men in leaving their homes and flocking to the colours is truly wonderful." One recalls such paragraphs, and one recalls visions of Wigan, St. Helens, Oldham and Sheffield.

True, the affections of man are strange and unreasoning, but the average home in such places is not calculated to inspire much love or loyalty or great self-sacrifice in its defence. That, of course, is the danger of letting one's country become *too* unpleasant—the dead point of indifference is passed and war (whether civil or other) is welcomed as at any rate a change from normal life.

The hundred per cent. pacifist should perhaps aim at a country which, purged of all causes for pride, love or enthusiasm, is yet not so utterly bereft of all attractions as to exasperate.

That is the sober norm towards which we are now trending. We are modifying both town and country, removing the worst reproaches from the one and much of its essential charm from the other.

We plant trees in the town and bungalows in the country, thus averaging England out into a dull uneventfulness whereby one place becomes much the same as any other—all incentive to exploration being thus removed at the same time as the great network of smoothed-out concrete roads is completed.

Truly it's an ill bird that fouls its own nest,

and not merely ill but perverted if it rejoices in the fouling.

The fact is that English people need mass psycho-analysis. We know the morbid symptoms—false standards and values, blindnesses and callousnesses and such-like. We need to discover the root causes of these disastrous abnormalities, and having discovered them, we may hope to prescribe for a cure. False values, and insensitiveness—particularly to beauty—these are probably at the root of the trouble.

Money itself has somehow usurped in our desires the place of the good things that it can purchase, or things good in themselves have crowded out of our limited imaginations the things which are better and best.

> " I often wonder what the vintners buy
> One half so precious as the things they sell."

Insufferably hackneyed as a quotation, how often does this doubt affect our actual lives?

Because natural beauty is so prodigal, because so much of it is free, we are in danger of disregarding it, like the air we breathe. It is perilously easy to lose all consciousness of it, to become inured and dead to its stimuli, as are most English people. As a fact of any significance in their lives it has ceased to exist, and talk about it seems to them just tedious and unrealistic.

Because the balance-sheets ignore the more real values, and chartered accountants apprehend them not, we too disregard them or treat them as amiably fictitious; so ludicrously topsy-turvy is the current evaluation of the practical, normal Englishman!

Yet the apprehension and contemplation of beauty have yielded and can still yield the most ecstatic pleasure of which humanity is capable. So complete an ecstasy may be rare—sharp, stabbing pleasure even may only visit us occasionally; but a happy awareness of beauty about us should and could be the everyday condition of us all.

" The beauty about us "—that is, the beauty of country, town and village, the normal visible setting of our ordinary everyday lives—not that which is mewed up in galleries and museums or between the covers of books.

It is this common background of beauty that this book seeks to champion and defend.

CHAPTER 3

OUR SHORT-SIGHTED FOREBEARS AND OUR
FUTILE SELVES

TO PRESCRIBE INTELLIGENTLY FOR CURATIVE
treatment, a careful diagnosis is the first
essential, based on a scrutiny and cataloguing of
the observable symptoms.

What, then, are the distressful symptoms of the
patient, England, and why, how, when and where
have they appeared?

From our point of view, England enjoyed almost
perfect health until the beginning of the last
century, when the first sporadic signs of a disfiguring malady began to show themselves here
and there in the busier and more populous parts
of the land. No doubt, time out of mind, there
had been occasional scars and sore places—mostly
ephemeral blemishes incidental to mining and
smelting, such as those from which Cornwall and
Sussex must have suffered whilst ours was still a
pastoral land.

But so slight and so few were these infantile

rashes that they affected the general complexion of the country not at all, whilst even the early intimations of an industrial future that the close of the eighteenth century vouchsafed to us were noticeable only as rare, if significant, portents, not as eruptions of any real or general importance in themselves.

In the old days, when a more or less spontaneous aggregation of people in some harbour or cross-roads town turned to production, it was in the people's own houses or workshops that the work was done, and there was little outward evidence of the industries they pursued. It was all on a very small scale, unsystematised, and not, by modern standards, very efficient in output per man hour.

With large-scale, specialised factory production under the impersonal and religiously materialistic control of joint-stock companies, things changed very rapidly even to the outer eye. As, in the Middle Ages, villages and towns grew up under the patronage and protection of the powerful abbeys and feudal castles, so in the nineteenth century did they spring up, bleakly, sombrely and formlessly, in the chill shadow of grim, Bastille-like factories.

It was no longer an old-established population choosing a craft—it was a new or transformed and centralised industry demanding a population at the factory gates to supply it with labour. The factory or the mine or the blast furnace— the counting-house—the timekeeper's lodge—the weigh-bridge—the great gates. At those great gates the companies' interest and responsibilities abruptly, arbitrarily and illogically ceased.

The employers kept clear an approach for their raw materials and an exit for their manufactures; and granted that, their operatives might live, not as they chose, but as they could, squalidly huddled near their work or squalidly sprawling abroad.

It was found that in return for a just non-starvation subsistence wage, labour was always sooner or later and somehow forthcoming, and that was that. Also it was an observed fact that this labour was sooner or later and somehow housed—usually exorbitantly, always meanly, and quite monstrously as regards amenity.

There was no attempt at an intelligent general lay-out plan; all was cut-throat grab, exploitation and waste—a mad game of beggar-my-neighbour between a host of greedy little sneak-builders and speculators—supplying the demand for homes meanly and usuriously, just as the Gradgrind employers supplied a quasi-subsistence.

It was nobody's business—it was the heyday of *laissez-faire;* and the remarkable results of that comfortable political philosophy are nowhere better exemplified than in some Victorian industrial area where, gaunt, grimy and forlorn, the workers' dwellings, whether singly, in terraces or in rows, huddle darkly in the hollows or sprawl haphazard about a desolate and treeless waste. To such places there is no centre, no articulate plan, no definite edge nor end: congested squalor thins out into sporadic squalor, and that in turn into grimy unkemptness, until at last the genuine agricultural country is reached—it is hard to say exactly where or when.

Take any square mile you like of semi-urban Black Country or of the industrial North or Midlands or the outer suburbs of almost any town—or take Peacehaven, or Waterlooville or Bournemouth, or an up-to-date ordnance survey map of the same areas. It is difficult to believe that the houses have been deliberately placed just *so* by thinking social animals—an untutored and charitable Martian would surely deride the idea, and suggest the more likely theory that the buildings had been caught by some tidy-minded wizard playing unauthorised blind-man's-buff in a bit of no-man's-land, and had been punished for their skittishness by being petrified on the instant just wherever they happened to stand.

For there they are—caught all higgledy-piggledy, and looking thoroughly lost and foolish, indeed, not knowing which way to look: " Mon Abri " stares vacantly at the shameful hinder parts of " Loch Lomond," which in turn is overlooked and put out of countenance by the baleful scowl of " Kia-Ora " on its flank. From their siting you would never guess that the sun rose quite dependably in the east, and set in the west, or that there was a prevailing wind, or that any one prospect was preferable to another—so little do their builders seem to have been guided by considerations of sunshine, shelter or view.

To do them justice, however, they do seem to have a general superstition that a building adjoining a road should be parallel to it—just as the orthodox are fidgeted by not being buried east and west. It is held to be proper to "face the road" (the "face" being the elevation with the front door and the bay windows); and this commandment, "Thou shalt face the road," and its almost universal acceptance, has resulted in the evolution of two utterly different styles of building, one for the front, which is the official public façade to be seen of all men, and the other for the sides and back, which, like dirty linen, are conventionally supposed to be for the family only.

But how do we find England as a whole to-day? Certainly she has changed alarmingly—is changing, and ever more rapidly, and the end is not yet.

What that end will be, no one knows and few, as yet, greatly care. That it will be what we choose to make it is certain, and we are not choosing well.

The conditions favouring the changes that have come upon us are scarcely new, either in kind or degree, nor unforeseen—or at any rate not unforeseeable. What are they?

A monstrously swollen population. Our steeply ascending birth-rate graph has been the pride and joy of our Jingo politicians for at least a century, and its trajectory could be calculated ahead with very tolerable accuracy.

The drift from agriculture to industry—from the

rural to the urban areas. That, too, is generations old and by no means incalculable.

Improved means of locomotion. Surely the shock of finding the flying coaches on Macadam's wonderful new roads quickly and suddenly superseded by the railways should have prepared us, or at any rate our rulers, for the possibility of revenge and a reversal, when concrete, rubber and petrol might turn the tables on steam and steel?

But no, we just say it's all very queer and unexpected and new, and above all difficult, and we struggle and muddle and tread on each other's toes and make the best of it in our wonderful British way, not by really grappling with it and getting things done, but by putting up with conditions intolerable to a people of spirit or imagination, and by telling ourselves comfortable lies about it all.

We say, " Things might well be worse "—they take us literally at our word and promptly *are*.

We are reputed to have, and no doubt actually have, the finest and most expensive Civil Service in the world. We do not lack records and statistics, we have all manner of data and surveys, we have a flexible legislature and a popularly elected Parliament. We write and sing quite a lot about " Old England," " Bonnie Scotland," " Land of my Fathers," and " The Emerald Isle "—not to mention " Glorious Devon," " Sussex by the Sea," and much more in that rather shy-making vein, and all with what naïve and self-deceiving insincerity! The " Men of Kent " may dine and wine together fraternally and patriotically, and the " Kentish Men " may toast each other as jolly good fellows, and Kent as the Garden of England, and the home of the Faire Maid, and the seat of the Primate and I know not what besides; but it is all sentimental unreality, and they will scarcely notice when the new collieries have made their county the back-yard of England—a new Southern Black Country—nor, alternatively, thank those who are valiantly striving to avert that measureless catastrophe should they by any means succeed.

As yet there is no general public opinion in favour of conservation, and that's the frightful and hamstringing truth.

If you have no sound and compelling public opinion, if, further, you have no leaders who will lead and no politicians with policies, your beautiful Civil Service and your accumulated data are of but little more use to you than are seven-league boots to a legless man.

So we wait for a sign and a stirring of the waters of indifference—whilst England perishes.

CHAPTER 4

SOME CAUSES OF URBAN BEASTLINESS, AND OF THE CONSEQUENT RUSH TO ESCAPE

IN ORDER TO ACCOUNT FOR THE PRESENT STATE of our older industrial towns—such places, for instance, as make up the Oldham–Manchester–Rochdale–Salford group—we have to try to get back into the state of mind of the time in which they were built.

In the period between 1830, when the pioneer cotton industrial area grew, and the 1870's, when the industrial revolution was practically complete, theory and practice went blithely hand-in-hand. Some people will say that this was because practice was urged forward by one of the most fundamental of human impulses, namely, greed, and that the classical economists did no more than rationalise what was already done. This rationalisation meaning, of course, no more than the subsequent finding of respectable reasons for what had already been determined upon on emotional grounds.

Anyhow, theory upheld the view that, in the eighteenth-century phrase, private vices were public benefits, and that if every man looked after himself, such vices as greed and avarice ultimately worked for efficiency and justice. Each man was expected to look after himself, and competition was supposed to protect the consumer. That is to say, if Smith in his avarice built bad houses or spun poor cotton, then Jones and Robinson ceased to deal with him, but took their orders to Brown, the rival builder or spinner. It was therefore not Smith's job to draw the line at unseasoned timber or faulty cloth. It was up to him to sell such goods if he could. It was the function of the consumer to catch him out if he could, and, if he did, to transfer his custom elsewhere.

There are few to-day who would say that this principle worked out very well even in the matter of cotton cloth; but in the matter of town-planning and housing it operated still worse. Under such a system the consumers' only safeguard was this very competition; but owing to facts of time and geography, that safeguard hardly worked at all when it came to building.

Let us consider for a moment how such industrial towns and villages as Oldham and its neighbours and satellites grew up.

All through the eighteenth century cotton-weaving had gone on in the valleys of these Lancashire moors. When cotton-spinning machinery was invented there were streams ready to turn it. Markets were discovered, and the demand for labour was sharp. It was as a rule no part of the system for the mill-owners themselves to provide housing for their operatives, or if they did they provided it, as it were, in their private capacity and as a side-line which they hoped to make profitable. Under the current system they were perfectly entitled to build as bad a house and charge as high a rent for it as they could get away with. If they did provide honest houses, it was as a work of supererogation, and they were under no obligation to do so; for in theory, at any rate, the operative was entirely free not to live in their houses if he thought them too bad.

Countless streets of mean houses on the grid plan were incontinently run up, no notice being taken of the contour of the ground or of existing trees or other amenities, each estate being developed quite independently of the other, usually without any drainage. The extent, by the way, to which our industrial towns are innocent of adequate drainage would be a surprise to those who have not personal knowledge of them.

When the speculator decided to run up his houses, he was usually able to buy his land quite cheaply, and his grid plan was often arranged fairly amply; so that each house had a longish strip of garden at the back of it—all the gardens forming a kind of square. But in days when there were no trams and no bicycles, the demand to be near the works was very great, and our speculator quickly found that all his houses were occupied, and that more were demanded.

The value of land had meantime gone up in the neighbourhood, and he saw that if he wanted to buy more of the land, whose value the growth of the town had appreciated, he must pay a very heavy price for it. He therefore cast his eye back on the plot that he already had, and found that either by building back to back with the original houses or by planning a little inner street down the middle of what used to be the gardens, he could do what was held to be his whole duty in life—that is, to double his income.

An incidental and unconsidered by-product of this intensive building was frequently a doubling of the death-rate also, especially amongst the unhappy children born into the narrow courts and alleys thus created.

The critics of such men and such methods—Morris, for example, and more particularly Ruskin—were inclined to be so shocked at the whole process that they could not consider it in detail; and Ruskin at any rate went so far as to condemn the very steam engine and the whirring wheels which had been its ultimate cause. But in this age we have almost forgotten that such protests were ever made, and we have the realism to believe that just as in a house there should be a kitchen, scullery, coal-hole and larder, and if possible a place with a carpenter's bench in it—so in the city there should be gas-works, gasometers, power stations, railway stations, factories and warehouses. Nor are Marinetti and Messrs. Brangwyn and Pennell alone in believing that factory chimneys, towering gantries, wharves and sheds and slag-heaps, pit-head winding gear, cranes and steel scaffolding, steamers and grain elevators, are all magnificent in their positive, truculent, modern way. It is good to see the human scale occasionally and valiantly transcended. It is good, in a soft town civilisation, to see fierce, uncouth monsters which can bring something of the grandeur of rock scenery into a tame landscape.

But go to almost any English industrial town—even to a comparatively reasonable, clean and prosperous place such as Barrow-in-Furness, and you will see that the trouble is that we are never quite sure what we want. We mix up the gigantic ogre-like beauty of our machines with ordinary human qualities, either by dolling up some engineering titan in irrelevant architectural fripperies that merely make it look a fool, or else by the actual physical juxtaposition of the giants with the homes of the people who are their servitors.

The woman who lives in the shadow of the rolling mills or the pithead in the pathetic little box which, once pink, is now black, will still put up her oblation of white lace curtains; still she, or her child, will try to grow a few geraniums; still she will cherish and polish until inside the cottage at any rate there is a semblance of the clean cheerfulness in which we all really desire to live.

The fact is that those who admire the macabre, and who draw it and extol it, do so first because they are not actually obliged to live with it, and only take an occasional excursion into its neighbourhood, or, secondly, they may actually be willing to live in the dirt and grime of the factory chimneys that they admire because they are already surfeited with more homely, human charms.

In a German inquiry into unsatisfactory industrial conditions, it was decided that one cause of dissatisfaction and fatigue was the noise and lack of charm in the factory buildings; and there has been a definite move all through the country not only to apply decent architectural standards in the new factories erected, but as far as possible to humanise them by planting them about with trees, grass and flowers. This was not done on humanitarian or philanthropic grounds (it is quite possible that it would have been better from those points of view to spend the money on an increase of wages), but because it seemed proved that beauty and seemliness in the factory buildings and surroundings really did promote industrial peace and efficiency.

But of course German industrialism gained very much by our experience. England was the pioneer industrial country; and though most of the other countries have made great mistakes in their industrial development, every one of those mistakes had been made previously and thoroughly in England. And in nothing has England suffered more from her position as a pioneer than in her reckless production of smoke.

Smoke is, of course, the *bete noire* of the architect. It coats his building with soot and a bituminous deposit, which ruins the mouldings, and, not content with that, erodes his projections till they are apt to look more like decayed teeth than architectural embellishments.

The Ministry of Health a few years ago calculated that six million pounds' worth of fuel a year is wasted in England on the production of worse than useless smoke. This was the mere waste of coal, and did not include the cost of extra washing which smoke causes in every town household, or the damage to agriculture, buildings and health.

Many experts, factory owners, heating engineers and so forth, seem agreed that smoke prevention is not only possible, even in England, but might well be directly profitable. There are a great many devices on the market for the prevention of industrial smoke; under one system twin boilers are used and coal is burned in one and coke in the other, the coal smoke being blown across the incandescent coke and consumed. In another an oil spray is forced across the top of the fire; in a third, use is made of a mechanical stoker.

Some, however, maintain that all that is needed are proper training and shorter hours for stokers.

This has certainly been the finding in industrial Germany. Stoking is a skilled job, but in England, at any rate, the stokers—all except the head men—are often completely unskilled. They work very long hours, moreover, and are naturally tempted to stoke seldom and excessively, with the natural result that their spasmodic ministrations are proclaimed by billowing clouds of poisonous smoke.

Unfortunately there seems to be no limit to the squalor that humanity will put up with in its ruthless, joyless, industrial towns, but there is a quite definite limit to the pollution of the air and the denial of sunlight below which life itself is not only prejudiced but actually endangered. Thus, quite apart from any reasonable human desire to live a little less ungraciously than is possible in the nastier of our towns, the very urge towards mere biological survival as an animal is forcing people out into the surrounding country.

In so far as the country is sought for its own delights, the instinct is clearly entirely right and laudable; but in so far as it is colonised by refugees fleeing from intolerable towns, who have no natural instinct for country life, but who elect to live there as it were negatively and under protest, for the sake of their own and their children's bodily and spiritual health, the movement is calamitous.

The social and cultural amenities of a civilisation can only be enjoyed to their full in a community

—a community of a certain size and compactness, that is, in a town; and no matter to what extent transport and communications may be improved, the town still remains essential to civilisation and the good life. What that town should be like, its schools, universities, clinics, galleries, museums, theatres, cinemas, public halls and such-like, as well as its industries and its optimum population —those are things about which some of us are much given to speculating. We speculate with the more freedom because clearly we have as yet nothing in England approaching the ideal, though we have at least one very gallant and promising experiment which will be referred to later.

But generally speaking we have latterly made such a mess and a muddle of our urban civilisation that had in many ways promised so well through the eighteenth century, that fewer and fewer people remain willing to put up with its unpleasantness for the sake of its cultural and social advantages. So, having made our towns with such careless incompetence, those of us who have the means to be choosers are calmly declining to live in them and are now proceeding with the same recklessness to disperse ourselves over the countryside, destroying and dishonouring it with our shoddy but all-too-permanent encampments.

Some, at any rate, of the *émigrés* really desire and would sincerely appreciate genuine country life in genuine unspoilt country, if they could by any means achieve it, and the exploiting and the cheating fulfilment of such aspirations by the speculator are truly pathetic.

As the Joneses fly from the town, so does the country fly from the pink bungalow that they have perched so hopefully on its eligible site. The true countryman will know that the area is infected—the Joneses have brought the blight of their town or suburb with them—and in all probability they and their home will be followed by an incursion of like-minded people similarly housed, and the country will be found to have further withdrawn itself beyond the skyline in its losing retreat towards the sea.

To do nothing but revile those who thus spoil the country with their nauseous little buildings, or merely to laugh darkly at their pathetic failure to achieve an imagined rusticity, is beautifully easy. But it is unjust, cynical and lazy—as though you were to curse a stricken family because in flying from its burning home it trespassed over your lawns and flower-beds.

What we must try to do is both to put out the fire—that is, to make town life not merely tolerable but attractive—and also to show how one may in very truth genuinely escape to and live in real country without offence and without thereby trampling underfoot and annihilating the very things that are so justly desired and so valiantly sought.

Let us first mitigate the shameful necessity for this diffusion of living and, having brought the thing within manageable bounds, let us so arrange things, so revise our laws and by-laws and public opinion, that the homes of the people are no longer disfiguring eruptions on the face of the land, but a welcome and becoming adornment, as they were in the days when England was beautiful because of them.

CHAPTER 5

NEW TOWNS FOR OLD

WHERE ONE'S AFFECTIONS ARE ENGAGED IT IS not easy to stand by and be the witness of outrage without giving way to maledictions as well as lamentations that are rarely helpful to a better state of things, whatever relief they may bring to the indignant individual.

However difficult, then, it is necessary to study the pertinent facts as dispassionately as may be. Three have already been mentioned—increased and increasing population, the industrialisation and urbanisation of the population, and improved transportation. These may well be examined a little more fully.

Birth control—possibly assisted by other agencies—is beginning to flatten out the trace of the birth-rate graph in a really encouraging fashion: the industrialisation graph is in a jerky patch and its future trend is obscure: whilst urbanisation has for some time been modified by and is now definitely yielding to suburbanisation, which, in its

the Octopus

turn, is due to—or at any rate is made possible by—improved transportation. The best authorities seem agreed with common-sense observation in this—that our island is inconveniently if not dangerously overcrowded; so that the decline in the birth-rate (not yet by any means in the *population*) is all to the good, whatever hard things the more austere of the bishops may have to say of birth control—and they are many. Feckless breed that we are, there had indeed been small hope for England without this tardy diminution in our fecundity. As things are, it is about the most heartening fact we can record.

The progressive decline of agriculture has, of course, accelerated industrialisation beyond its own intrinsic increment, making both new problems and the old problems more acute, and reducing the country to something perilously like a desert studded with wide-spreading industrial, business, residential and mining oases.

The present sudden and largely unforeseen state of chaos and unemployment in coal-mining and some of the old heavy industries almost certainly precedes and presages great changes—changes for better or worse—in the very aspect of England as well as in the lives of millions of men and women. It may even be that a deserted and bankrupt Black Country shall be cast derisively back at us in the cold, disillusioning light of " the morning after." No longer drunk with the hazards and prizes of industrial gambling—the grim casino silent and the tables overturned—we shall see perhaps for what it is, this place we made, or suffered to be made, as the home and nursery for ten millions of our countrymen.

There was one thing only that made life just supportable in such places—the lure of wages. As they are, remove that one attraction—the means of living (more or less)—and no one will stay there who can get away.

But getting away means having somewhere to go to, and there are no empty homes anywhere, so that the ten millions must needs for the most part stay where they are and survey the ruins.

"Survey the Ruins"—why only the unhappy and innocent victims? Why not a Government Department? *Literally* survey them, with theodolite and measuring staff—the whole of our shameful, ramshackle squalordom: a band of surveyors, town planners, architects, foresters and gardeners, followed by artisans and labourers enrolled *ad hoc* from the unemployed inhabitants of the shameful places, pledged to remove the reproach and to make them tolerable?

The breath that gave life, the same blasted what it made; and where the mines and furnaces and foundries are closed down, there is some hope for regeneration and the introduction of civilised amenities. It is a chance to be taken. The time for "alterations and improvements" is during changes of management and in the slack season.

A stricken town cannot lightly be deserted: therefore it must be improved and made ready for, and worthy of, a new and different future. With good communications, its existing public services—water, light, power, sewers, etc.—its public buildings and schools, and above all with improved housing, new industries will be attracted and employment will be found.

If in the meantime the population has dwindled, so much the better for the place: it can be shorn of its unhealthy overgrowth and reduced to a compact and orderly township, perhaps with a park in place of its old slum area, and with a fair green belt of fields and trees girdling it about instead of its old untidy fringe of dilapidated works and slatternly shacks and dwellings.

Private ownerships, vested interests and finance would all be difficult to deal with—obviously—but it could be done. It would mean Parliamentary powers, large loans and heroic measures generally; but it could be done. The worst of heroic measures, however, is that they need heroes to carry them through; and heroes mostly seem content with just demanding a land fit for heroes to live in. It is not the sort of thing you can ring for and have brought you on a silver tray, yet too many do nothing at all—except ring.

Save, of course, at places like Welwyn. But Welwyn is so scandalously unique that few even of those who have heard of it really grasp what it is, what it has done and what it stands for.

If it were typical of England, instead of being quite startlingly exceptional, we should indeed be in a different plight; and depressing little books such as this could only appear as a morbid kind of fiction—picturing an inverted Utopia such as Dante, Butler and Swift might have jointly concocted.

What, then, is this Welwyn, this paragon of a place, this town unique—or almost unique—in all England?

It is an humiliating admission, but it is just plain common-sense, foresight and good management, and nothing else. And so it is unique, and so it is becoming a by-word and a wonder, and so it is comely and spacious, prosperous and healthy.

Perhaps the best definition that can be given of the idea of the garden city or village is that it is functional. The object of its founders is not to make a profit, but to provide for certain recognised human needs.

It is well known, for instance, that a church, a school, a shop and a burial-ground will be wanted for every so many thousand inhabitants. These simple needs were as a rule provided by the old village; but recent years have somewhat lengthened the list of our requirements. In the case of a garden city, football and cricket fields, children's playgrounds, a municipal golf-course, tennis-courts, and an assembly hall will be all wanted, as also, of course, a cinema and theatre, besides the buildings proper to the educational, health, municipal and other public services.

Even at Baku, one of the most remote industrial towns in all Russia, this is thoroughly understood and acted upon so far as the limited resources of the Soviets will allow. Here on the barren shores of the Caspian and the farthest edge of Europe, amongst oil gushers, sledges, fire-worshippers, veiled women, and camels, the barbaric, common-sense Russians are doing as a matter of course very much what we are so proud of having accomplished at Letchworth, Welwyn and the Hampstead Garden Suburb.

Then it has been computed how much road and rail accommodation is on an average required for the service of so many thousands, while their needs in water, gas, electricity, and drainage and so forth can be accurately gauged.

Further, a fairly calculable proportion of them will be willing or anxious to engage in industry if such work is forthcoming.

Starting, then, from these very simple facts, which can be known or guessed about people, it is possible to compile a town far more economically and agreeably than on the old principle of haphazard growth described in an earlier chapter.

In the ideal garden city the land or building estate belongs to the community, which takes care that it shall not grow beyond a size in which all its inhabitants can have easy access to the country. The ground-rents, and the profits on all public services, go back to the community, so that rates can be kept low. As the whole of the land already belongs to the town, there can be no profiteering or squeezing if, for instance, it should decide that it needed a new playing-field.

If the population increases considerably, the community can decide whether it will found a satellite village outside the carefully preserved agricultural belt, or whether it is expedient to allow expansion to continue within the belt, and if so precisely to what extent.

Above all, the old uncongenial juxtaposition of factory and dwelling-house can be avoided. No heavy traffic need rack the nerves of the residential quarter; no glowering gasometer will browbeat the pleasant little houses, but grass and trees will crown the hills, the very streets themselves will be as gardens, and after due provision has been made for wharves and water-carriage generally, the rest of the river will be made accessible and greenly welcoming for the pleasure of the people.

Besides this, there will be cohesion in the architectural scheme, and even if the community is comparatively poor and the garden city is adorned by no striking public buildings, still charm and seemliness can be assured—the charm, seemliness and essential rusticity which the poor bungalow dwellers try to get, and of which their own ignorance and the rapacity of the speculators so cruelly cheat them.

CHAPTER 6

THE TRAGIC FOLLY OF CASTLE MALORY

HAVING GLANCED AT WELWYN, REPRESENTATIVE of the handful of similarly "intentional" communities, let us look at the overwhelming majority—the *laissez-faire* towns of England.

The following is a composite portrait of several places and typical of many. We will call it Castle Malory. Innocent people have actually journeyed thither not on business, attracted by its pleasant-sounding name; because it is mentioned in Doomsday Book, and because of a certain de Malory who won mild celebrity in the Wars of the Roses. Also it looks rather inviting on the map, situated as it is at the head of a navigable river estuary, with a deep gorge behind it running back amongst the hills of a romantically tumbled hinterland.

Such tourists have, however, grown fewer and fewer: they have never returned themselves, nor have they ever counselled anyone else to make the journey.

In short, the " gaff " of Castle Malory has been effectually and finally " blown."

What, then, is wrong with the place? To put it briefly—just everything; everything, that is, except its site.

To begin with, there isn't any castle. There was until 1856—or, rather, the shell of the keep and the inner bailey and barbican—an imposing and exceedingly picturesque group of ruins, to judge from old aquatints of a few years earlier. They were demolished to make way for the depot barracks, designed and built by the Royal Engineers. The designing and building of Royal Engineers are scarcely distinguishable from those of railway engineers; and remembering Vauban and Mansart and Louis XIV you would scarcely guess them to be royal at all.

As to architecture, at Castle Malory at any rate, distinctly the railway has it, the station building of blue bricks striped with yellow being on the whole less violently repulsive than the barracks of yellow bricks striped with blue. And besides being less hugely livid than the 1856 barracks, one has less resentment against the 1860 station in that it fulfilled a more urgent and reasonable demand, and its site was chosen, if foolishly, at any rate less high-handedly. True, it has obliterated the old shipyard and adjoining water-meadows, and the railway line has cut off the town from its old water-front; and " Pilots' Row "—a jumble of tall, narrow-fronted, bow-windowed houses by the old jetty—has been demolished to enlarge the goods yard.

Also the unusually ugly railway bridge spanning the river entirely cuts off what, according to early water-colours and a traveller's journal of 1801, was "a view picturesque rather than sublime, the steep banks of the curving river with their hanging beech woods opening out towards the sea and the setting sun, framed on the one hand by the ruins of the castle perched high above the red roofs and smoke-reek of the town, on the other by the tall masts of merchantmen docked within the shelter of Barton's Bluff."

The picture post-cards you can now buy at the cash chemists in Castle Street show nothing at all like that. Gone alike are the tall masts and the beech trees, the castle, and the view of the river's mouth. You may buy a post-card of Castle Street that no longer leads to the castle—of Victoria Avenue with never a tree in all its tedious length—of the Jubilee fountain that has been dry these thirty years—of Inkerman Gardens, where horticulture is confined to variegated laurels, seemingly of an extraordinary rarity, to judge by the forbidding railings that defend them.

Other post-cards show the War Memorial, which, because it is mostly angel and not tin hats, and because you have not yet despaired of the arts, you guess is South African. It isn't.

Then there is the Mayor's Park, a composition in cast iron and asphalt, grimy rockeries and Public Conveniences for Ladies and Gentlemen.

Le Notre or Watteau or Capability Brown, indeed, would be completely deceived—their idea of a park was something so much less evolved.

The quite new co-operative stores is a valiant affair conceived in variegated glazed bricks and immense sheets of plate-glass—the largest in the town and the pride of the excellent manager. Behind a completely blackguard facade is a well-planned lay-out in which honest business is efficiently conducted.

The Salvation Army barracks have a childishly castellated front that may, one hopes, be equally deceptive.

There is no deception about the Police Station: it looks its job to a hair, and hence, according to a certain school of critics, must be good architecture. To those who know the Castle Malory Police Station the alternative occurs—such may be bad critics.

High Street has aggrandised itself out of all knowing and out of all order and seemliness. Only some three or four of the old parapeted Georgian fronts still stand with their rosy brickwork and white-sashed windows, and in all but one of these, great sheets of plate-glass have replaced the original shop fronts with their carefully proportioned panes that were also good shopkeeping. In such, instead of being as it were emptied out into the street in negligent display, the wares, but half revealed, sparsely and almost coyly, entice one within for their fuller realisation and achieve the tradesman's first object of getting one actually into the shop and within the range of his salesmanship.

This principle seems to be fully grasped by the best shopkeepers on the Continent and in America, and to some extent in London; but the plate-glass façade is still a fetish in the provinces.

It is chiefly the unbridled yet futile individualism of the shopkeepers, as expressed in their buildings, that has turned the urbane old High Street into pandemonium—though the rot began with the mid-Victorian post office, a preposterous ineptitude in Anglo-Venetian Gothic. This reared its fretful terra-cotta gable a full two stories above the old cornice line of the street that architectural good manners had until then kept almost unanimously broken. Those who know Buols' Restaurant at Oxford can picture the disastrous effect, at once disruptive and crushing, of Castle Malory's post office.

Fortunately, however, the plan is as inept as the elevation, and so inadequate are the pedantic Gothic windows, so awkward and cranky the whole building, that the post office has at last abandoned it in despair and removed to brand-new and quite admirable premises along the street—a suave, clean-lined building of pleasant brick, with little ornament beyond the finely-carved keystones to the big arched windows.

It is one of the two wholly satisfactory buildings in the town: the other is a bank. Indeed, certain of the great banks and H.M. Office of Works, that now designs the post offices and telephone exchanges, have set an architectural example that multiple stores would do well to follow. Some of the banks, particularly, make a genuine and often successful attempt to harmonise themselves with what is best and most characteristic in the particular towns they serve—being adaptably willing either to fall into line with a group of gravely urbane Georgian neighbours or elsewhere to emulate the more romantic fashions of a Tudor *vis-à-vis*.

Will the day ever come when one could say that of cash chemists, or boot stores, or multiple dairies or grocers? At present these powerful and all-pervading combines are architecturally no better than the local tradesmen and little one-man stores, more often worse. It is odd that their boards of directors should seemingly contain no solitary man—or, at any rate, not enough men—sufficiently civilised or imaginative, or even with sufficient pride, to see to it that their business is housed, if not with some distinction, at least with less gimcrack vulgarity.

Or perhaps it is not odd. . . .

Anyway, commercial enterprise has done wonders for poor old Castle Malory, and reduced it from being a country town of real distinction and quite unusual amenity almost to the average English level of urban insipidity and tediousness, than which there are few lower.

True, a good deal of the misguided enterprise has come from its own foolish citizens. Landon Park—the lodge gates of which are scarcely ten minutes' walk from the Town Hall—was offered to the corporation by its late owner at its agricultural value, together with its famous beech-woods clothing the steep river banks right up to the town at half their timber valuation. The only stipulation was that the place (except for some twenty acres) was not to be built upon, but kept as a public open space for the town of Castle Malory for ever—the beech-woods and riverside walks being properly maintained.

The fine Palladian mansion and its gardens and temples were to be thrown in; the owner expressing the wish that the house might be retained as a museum or a municipal sports club or school or hospital, or some other public institution, but not making this conditional.

The acceptance of this public-spirited offer would have meant something like a penny on the rates. But it was refused—and what has happened?

The owner died intestate, and the whole property had to be liquidated. The town had already made itself too unpleasant a place for anyone with means and a free choice to settle deliberately on its outskirts, and there were no bids at the auction for the property as a whole. The two or three outlying farms were soon afterwards disposed of, and an offer from a speculating land dealer was subsequently accepted for the house, the park and beech-woods.

The speculator resold the woods and even the trees in the park to a timber merchant, who forthwith felled all that were worth while, leaving a ragged and dishevelled wilderness, whilst the house he sold to a builder for demolition. Having made his profit by these two transactions, and having reduced Landon Park to a desert, he was prepared to let it go at prairie value, and at such it was bought in four lots by four more little speculators.

Each of these parcelled out his own purchase into building plots in his own quite futile fashion, with no attempt at co-ordination or a general idea; and each sold quite an encouraging number of sites. Then it became generally known that the land was too high to be served reliably by the existing town water supply, and that there would be difficulties about drainage. It was likewise gradually realised that what had seemed such a desirable situation in the old days before the trees had gone was now not only exceedingly forlorn-looking but intolerably bleak and wind-swept, and also that land that had looked fertile enough under the bracken and rough grass of the old park was in reality quite useless for gardening.

So only here and there—rather than cut their losses—a few purchasers, hardier than the rest, erected the poor half-hearted bungalows we see to-day, *sans* roads, *sans* water, *sans* drains, *sans* everything. The rest of that tussocky waste and shattered woodland still awaits a purchaser, though unless Castle Malory should suddenly find a need to grow again quite seriously one cannot imagine what use it could be put to.

Poor old Castle Malory—and poor citizens, if they only knew it! The town that was so comely and welcoming, nestling in its woods with its feet in the shining sea—how tragically have its charms and its amenities been filched and frittered away!

First the railway elected to approach and enter the town most mischievously up the left shore of the estuary, so denying the citizens their direct and immemorial access to the sea.

This approach also meant that the railway had to be carried across the river to its goods terminus at the dock on the opposite bank, so truncating the estuary itself and hindering up-river traffic, as well as destroying the famous view.

And that when the line should obviously have been brought along the other and quite dull side of the estuary and have ended at the docks, with a graceful road bridge thence across to the town.

It would have been easier and more direct for the railway company; but some vested interest " got at " somebody, and the line was disastrously built as we find it.

Had it been otherwise, the fine sands and the town's old repute would have ensured its prosperity as a place for residence or holidays; whereas it now subsists precariously as a dying port and a market, and on its rapidly declining industrial interests to which it gave itself so rashly, inadvisedly and unreservedly.

Now, after passing two or three dismal little works that have failed and a peppering of squalid little houses huddling between the railway embankment and the water's edge, you enter the town between its twin malodorous guardians, the gasometers and the sewage works.

From the shabby station the traveller steps into an untidy waste of greasy cobbles, surrounded by a few gaunt and dejected shops and great hoardings blown somewhat askew that are not even crudely gay with posters, as half of them are " To Let." Not a blade of grass, not a tree, not a flower—not even a basket for the waste-paper and orange-peel that litter the arena.

" Station Road " is station road *à l'Anglaise*, but one hopes there may not be much of it and that the town itself will be very different; but one is disappointed. The visitor may perhaps remember some panegyric in his old guide-book of the walks through the hanging woods or the view down the river. Both are gone.

Or he may have heard of the sunken lane to Saddler's Ring. The lane is still there, though widened and shorn of its gnarled and arching oaks, whilst inquisitive bungalows now stare down into what were its secret and shadowed depths. The Ring itself, being a scheduled antiquity, has not been built upon ; but it has been fenced round with red spiked railings. And why not ? Who would wish to go there now ?

The old guide-book further recommends one to apply at the lodge for a permit to view the gardens and the long avenue at Landon Park. We already know the abomination of desolation that has fallen on that gracious place.

Then what is there to charm or beguile one in Castle Malory? A romantic past? An industrious if philistine present? It is not enough—we have already stayed over-long, and we will leave the unhappy place by the next train with the blinds drawn down—for ever.

CHAPTER 7

THE ARCHFIEND AND THE ARCHANGEL

WHEN CURSING THE PHILISTINE AND ALL HIS works, one is sometimes asked by the less dissatisfied, " Well, what *is* it all about ? What exactly is the matter and who's to blame, and what's to be done about it, anyway ? "

To such scatter-gun questions this whole book is an attempted answer; but it may serve to define the sort of actions that seem to be disastrous to amenity and generally anti-social if we invent a hypothetical person—an ideal monster of stupidity and greed—and so, as it were, dramatise the infelicities from which we suffer as though they were his individual misdeeds.

This fictional character, then, whom we will call Mr. Otherman, is a substantial citizen—a member of various local government bodies and a person of great activity. He prides himself on being practical and hard-headed, and has no patience at all with " all this art stuff." Yet there is a striking portrait of him by G. F. Watts in the Compton Gallery. It is called "Mammon."

In the black book of the recording angel the naughtiness of Mr. Otherman is thus discursively set down.

Firstly. "As a young man you took advantage of an unusually wet winter to buy a flooded riverside field cheap, and advantage of a dry summer a few years later to sell it for cottage building at a very handsome profit.

"The cottages have always been damp and unhealthy, and a beautiful water-meadow, from across which the famous view of the Norman Abbey used to be seen from the bridge, has been turned into a ragged slum.

"You knew that excellent building land was readily available elsewhere, but with a speculating builder as your accomplice you could not resist this perfectly legal opportunity of turning a dishonest penny.

"You are not alone in your guilt. None of the authorities concerned should have permitted houses to be built in such a situation: the town council or the Abbey guardians should have secured the meadow at its low agricultural value as a permanent open space for the amenity of the place and the pleasure of its inhabitants and all who passed that way.

"The world and your fellows are in this the worse for your living.

Secondly. "For your own ends, and because you had secretly and shrewdly bought up long road frontages on the main town approaches, you ridiculed the council's nascent interest in town planning, with the result that in order to reach the open country it is now necessary to pass your calamitous villas for a weary mile of unrewarded walking whichever route be taken. This has largely destroyed the remaining amenity of the town, and has raised the rates by reason of the expensive drainage and other public services entailed by this malformation of the town by 'tentacle growth.'

"You enriched yourself at the expense of your birthplace, and the world and your fellows are the worse for your living.

Thirdly. "The traffic capacity of the town's historic approaches having been greatly reduced by your ribbon development and the consequent car parking along either side, the provision of a wide new road into the town through an undeveloped patchwork of allotments was forced upon the authorities.

"Having been once bitten, certain far-sighted councillors proposed that this new road at least should be preserved as a seemly entrance to the town and be treated as a 'Park-way'—that is, with the open land lying on either side kept free from buildings except of a public or monumental nature—and laid out as a park or pleasaunce with grass and trees and flowers.

"Your mean little mind could not conceive that a free gift even from the town to itself could actually be 'good business,' and that such a liberal policy would pay good dividends in cash as well as in happiness. So you engineered and stimulated the pinchbeck opposition, and still more of your shoddy shops and base little houses grimace at each other across the road that should have passed graciously through a welcoming space of green.

"You even scotched the proposal for planting this road as an avenue as a silly and sentimental waste of space and money, and it now takes a man (or a woman or a child) a full fifteen minutes' walking before a tree may be found to sit under.

"You have filched away the birthright of your townsmen, and they and the world are the worse for your living.

Fourthly. "Having by this time got yourself more than a little disliked by certain of the older and more influential inhabitants, and having appreciably lowered the tone and quality of the whole town, you decided to move out. You naïvely sought to rehabilitate yourself in your neighbours' esteem by a book-entry rise in the social scale.

"You purchased the historic old house and park of Abbots End, just clear of the town, and with it the Lordship of the Manor.

"Your new way of life, however, failed of its objects, and you found ridicule now added to contempt. Your mortified wife applauded your piqued resolve to sell out and quit, but you found that the classy decorations and improvements on which you had spent so much had actually and very sharply reduced the market value of the old manor-house.

" You had not even the sense or imagination to exploit the property to the best advantage, but squandered its potentialities by your greedy rule-of-thumb retailing, regardless of all amenity.

" You are a fool as well as a knave, and the world and your fellows are the worse for your living.

Fifthly. " Having so signally failed in your rôle of Country Gentleman, and having taken your mean revenge on all that had supported your empty claim to that pretension, you bought a slice of Downland on the coast, where you built yourself an appropriate villa that hallooed its challenge in a strident Cockney voice over three miles of rolling downs, the sheer white cliffs and the defenceless sea.

" From this decoy house you looked upon your land and saw that it was good—good for exploitation—' Ripe for development.'

" So you formed a syndicate of like-minded persons and set up an imposing office in London, and advertised your scheme so handsomely in the Press that even some of the less suspect London ' dailies ' felt bound to speak kindly of your enterprise.

" You did not scruple to tempt two or three qualified but struggling doctors to write extravagant eulogies of your subsoil, of your water (of which there was very little), and of your air, which was of the ordinary quality. There was a great deal about ozone and the dancing waves sparkling in the limpid sunlight, which was partly and sometimes true: nothing about drainage—which was wise, as there wasn't any—little about roads, for a similar reason, little specific indeed about any public services or obligations, but a great deal of heady innuendo that the Garden of Eden was at hand.

"Your prospectus writer was honest to this extent: he gave you a cyclonic puff in exchange for his fee.

"Your artists and publicity agents were similarly conscientious. Also they were skilful, and managed to convey just what was wanted without recourse to downright lying or actionable misrepresentation, which was exactly what you wanted.

"Little drawbacks and awkwardnesses were tactfully ignored or glossed over. The fact that the crumbling cliffs cut off access to the beach almost entirely, and were themselves a perpetual danger, was skilfully evaded. That the beach when reached consisted of a slimy ooze (the disquieting smell being, of course, the abnormally powerful ozone as advertised), was not thought of sufficient general interest to mention, any more than the fact that a dangerous current sweeps over a treacherous quicksand a cable's length from the shore.

"The artist's engaging pictures were prudently entitled 'Seaville as it will be,' 'The proposed shopping centre,' 'The games reservation—as planned,' 'Sketch for the cliff gardens,' and so forth.

"No, you couldn't be caught on those. Nor were you ever caught; though you were severely frightened by the indignant clamour that presently arose from your unhappy dupes.

"Even to this day Seaville is a reproach and a byword for all that is short-sighted, wasteful, predatory and stupid in capitalistic speculation.

"So grasping and get-rich-quick were you and your associates that your over-stimulated goose began to pine and die after the first season's egg-laying, and so little did you do about fulfilling your obligations as implied by your 'propaganda' that more than half the plots sold remain unbuilt upon to this day.

"You found five thousand acres of Downland pasture—the immemorial resort of peaceful wanderers from the adjacent towns: you left it a forlorn and straggling camp of slatternly shacks and gimcrack bungalows, unfinished roads and weather-beaten advertisements.

"You brought chaos out of order, you created Golgotha-on-Sea, you acted blasphemously, and the world and your fellows are the worse for your living.

Sixthly. "Whilst on the crest of your short-lived Seaville boom you cut something of a figure in the less reputable financial circles of the City, and found yourself the chairman of 'Hope's Motor-Tyre Rejuvenating Fluid, Ltd.,' and 'Faith's Complexion Requisites, Inc.'

"You had acquired a taste and discovered an aptitude for 'selling publicity' for not-quite-technically-fraudulent advertisement, and you personally directed the propaganda work of both concerns. You hired blank walls and urban hoarding space by the acre, which was relatively unobjectionable, but you had a number of bright ideas of your own, which were not.

"You bought a fifty-acre pasture on the slopes of the Berkshire downs where these rise steeply up from the railway and the Western road, and within a month the ancient turf had been flayed away to form great white letters in the underlying chalk some twenty feet high, spelling out the names and virtues of your questionable nostrums.

"You hired the roofs of barns all over the South and Midlands from unprosperous farmers, and stencilled your own praises thereon in yellow and white distemper: you did the same on the tawny sails of the Thames barges, and upon gasometers and railway bridges all up and down the country.

"Along the main trunk roads your enamelled iron advertisements were bolted to every gate, in every field the monstrous effigy of a motor wheel and a toilet mirror proclaimed your horrid wares.

"In the summer holidays you would announce each morning in the newspapers, on what particular Welsh mountain top or near what Lakeland solitude or Highland fastness your famous white and yellow casket might be sought for, containing a £10 coupon for the finder. Your precious casket would be found, and scores of empty beer-bottles, cart-loads of paper, would remain as mute witnesses of the quantity and quality of the treasure-seekers.

"To the existing whips of the garage advertisements you added your own scorpions: you became IT in 'progressive advertising,' no congress of puff-mongers was complete without you, and you even had hopes of joining the Knights Bachelor of that profession, when the crash came.

"You were really a generation too late, and you had reckoned without the Scapa [1] Society, whose protests you had derided.

"Through its beneficent machinations you were brought low—you and your discredited companies—partly by a special Act of Parliament which wrecked your grandiose advertising system, and left you with crippling liabilities, but chiefly by the spirited though belated action of the public, who supported a boycott of all your products with a unanimity and thoroughness not to have been guessed at from their former long-suffering silence.

"You were carried away and at last destroyed by your own cunning: you had antagonised the Press by failing to advertise adequately in the newspapers, where, as at railway stations, advertisements are both effective and welcome, and

[1] Scapa Society for prevention of disfigurement in town and country, 7 Buckingham Palace Gardens, S.W. 1.

they had no compunction in hounding on the public to your well-deserved destruction.

"In this matter, though you made England almost uninhabitable for two nightmare years, your very excesses so frightened the more enlightened of the public, that outrages on anything like the same scale or of comparable offensiveness have been made for ever impossible.

"Thus, though in this your intentions were vile and your sins were as scarlet, the world and your fellows are the *better* for your living.

"But don't think you get any marks for THAT."

And there, at the moment, the Recording Angel's Otherman *dossier* abruptly ends—with a postscript that the subject of it is in process of changing his name.

By the time this extract is printed there is certain to be some fresh outrage or atrocity that we shall recognise as the work of this versatile hydra. It is already suggested that Mr. Blair Sackville-Egerton, who has recently established himself in Piccadilly as "The Spa and Coastal Resort Bureau," is none other than our old friend under his latest *alias*. He is an Advertising Consultant, Town Booster and Land Boomer, and unobtrusively, himself a considerable real-estate speculator.

He has chosen the most promising field for his talents, and should do well. Most of the watering-places will love him.

CHAPTER 8

DONKEYS, DRONES AND OSTRICHES

THE AIM OF THE LAST CHAPTER WAS TO SET hair on end, flesh creeping and blood curdling or even boiling. A faulty incantation may have robbed the spell of these horrid effects, and in that case the author is alone to blame.

If, however, anyone can actually witness such deeds as were described without grief and indignation, or even, unmoved, imagine them for himself, then that person must blame himself or his defective understanding or his unfortunate upbringing, and either try to educate his social and æsthetic conscience up to civilised normality or know himself for one of those rare unfortunates—a social and æsthetic imbecile.

The careful reader will have remarked that though the last chapter more or less fulfilled its promise of outlining " What's wrong," it barely touched on " Who's to blame and What's to be done about it." That, of course, is the more difficult part, also the more useful if one can happen on anything like a true view. At best it can only be roughly and partially true.

Who, then, are to blame?

The Othermans of this world are already indicted, but Everyman is answerable. What early training do we give young Everyman, that he may understand this responsibility laid upon him and bear it with competence and honour?

What of the Board schools, the secondary, preparatory and public schools—what are they doing?

What that is helpful, in this regard, is taught in the numberless Art Schools where, in buildings of unnerving ugliness, plaster casts, daffodils and nudes bound the æsthetic horizon of their votaries?

The answer is, little or nothing; and that is one of the things we are all to blame for, from the Minister of Education downwards.

If one must have school prayers—or, rather, if it were proved that such had any general effect at all of the kind intended—and if the things we are dealing with were ever regarded with seriousness, surely a prayer for the apprehending and making of civic beauty would not be out of place.

If prayer avail, let us then pray for the apprehending, making and guarding of Beauty, and more especially for the state of England:

> " Lighten our darkness, we beseech thee, that we behave ourselves seemly in our works and defile not the land that is for the delight and use of all men.

"Show to the fool his folly, that he may no more build wantonly after the vain imagination of his dark and lonely heart, doing both ill for himself and a great mischief to his fellows.

"Show him a little wisdom, that he may first ponder well and take counsel with the understanding, remembering them of old who wrought faithfully.

"Let him honour his town and his country, let him regard his neighbour and his neighbour's view, and build not vaingloriously, but in honesty, a house meet to his proper needs and meet to the place where it stands.

"We pray that he that buildeth or that maketh a road or that planteth or felleth a tree or doth aught else to change the face of this our country, may have a right guidance in all things, lest haply the beauty and the glory of the land be utterly destroyed, so that our children's children shall know it not, yet shall rise up and curse us for unfaithful stewards who, getting and spending, laid waste their heritage.

"Grant us the love of beauty, without which it cannot come; the desire for wisdom, without which our labours and our love are vain.

Amen."

As to the schools, the first thing to do is to educate the educational authorities, then to interest and teach the teachers. The only spur or carrot for High Authority is public opinion expressed through the Press and the ballot box.

Support a newspaper that is sound and active about amenities—if you can find one—and give your vote to the parliamentary, county council or municipal candidate who seems the least brutishly regardless of the things you care for.

Then it may be that our children's children may yet behold a party with an actual amenity policy, promising to do something, meaning to do something and—ultimately—doing something.

What is wrong with the Conservative party is that it seeks to conserve the wrong things, with the Liberals and Radicals that they are respectively neither, with the Communists that all Marx and no Morris has made them dull boys, and with all of them that they don't care because they haven't thought—because the constituencies haven't made an effective demand because *they* haven't thought, expressibly, nor been instructed; which brings us back to the schools, the beginning and end of every circle, vicious or virtuous.

Perhaps the likeliest way of breaking into this circle is through the schoolmasters and schoolmistresses themselves, who are, on the whole, zealous for education in its wider sense and about the most generally enlightened class in the community. If they will, the teachers can do much in the cause of amenity, even without official instructions.

They can teach their pupils that it is ill-mannered, unneighbourly and filthy to leave litter of any sort about; that orange-peel, wastepaper and the like, indecently exposed, are marks of the beast. They should analyse their locality, pointing out generally what is seemly or beautiful and why, and what is mean, ugly and uncivilised. They should try to set up a standard of visual decency and amenity by showing and describing what exists and what has been done in other places and in other countries, thus combating not merely indifference but any unwarrantable complacence.

If the schoolmasters and schoolmistresses do their work well, most English children will be thoroughly dissatisfied with their surroundings and with their elders' messy muddling, which is why there will be but little pressure on teachers from their directors or paymasters to do any such thing as has been suggested.

So the teachers must meanwhile do what good they can by stealth, and, after all, what could sound less dangerous than a series of talks on, say, "Population," "Housing," "Town Planning," "Transportation," "Architecture," "Scenery," "Tidiness," "Neighbourliness," "Health," "Local Government" and "Arboriculture"?

Are there any of these subjects that could not shelter under the wide umbrella of "Citizenship" with perfect honesty—a course on which could scarcely be objected to as subversive?

In a Cambridgeshire village a new type of school

known as the Village College is being initiated by Mr. Henry Morris, the Secretary for Education in that county. In it elementary school teachers and their pupils will be brought into closer contact than hitherto with those who are or will be responsible for local affairs, and by this means the pupils of the college will begin to take an intelligent interest in some of the subjects suggested in the foregoing paragraph. Once this interest has been aroused, a sense of responsibility for local affairs will assuredly follow.

One would have supposed that the Churches, being nominally concerned with spiritual values and the good life, and not being bound to show prospective money dividends like a joint-stock company, or lowered rates or other purely material advantages like a Borough Council, would have had something to say on such matters; but one would have supposed wrongly.

The average minister of religion, as one might expect, is temperamentally an antiquary and an historian rather than a pioneer and a reformer. He is not generally given to preaching discontent, and the kind of person likely to respond actively if he did is not given to church-going.

There is in England too much respect for persons and for vested interests and too little respect for beauty and for unauthorised happiness—the bleak legacy of the Reformation and the Puritans. It has taken a good half-century of protest and propaganda effectively to restrain the English clergy from destroying their own beautiful churches by half-baked antiquarian " restoration "; though, to be sure, the Victorian architects were no better than the parsons. Indeed, the truth probably is that a generation or so ago the clergy were no more blind or vandal than anyone else; and it is only relatively that they seem worse to-day. Or perhaps it is merely that one expected something from them, that one had imagined they might be able and eager to give—only to find it was " not in their line " and " not stocked."

Quite possibly they are right and know their own business, which one gathers must be very rigorously restricted by its Articles, as otherwise so likely and rewarding a side-line as the championship of " daily bread seemliness " would scarcely be neglected in this period of ecclesiastical slump.

With a few quite brilliant exceptions, University Dons can, from our point of view, be classed little higher than the clergy. Considering their guaranteed intelligence (which, however, is often special rather than general) and their contact with ideas, with the humanities and (at Oxford and Cambridge at any rate) with an environment of great beauty, this insensitiveness or, more strictly, this irresponsiveness is rather disturbing. Most of them, one imagines, must be more or less gratefully aware of the surrounding loveliness, though perhaps too much in the archæological and historical mood. They accept it—they approve of it—but they feel no impulse or obligation to make sure that it does not perish away, or to increase it or to spread it abroad throughout their so otherwise England.

" There is nothing for it to-day, if you have an appetite for the beautiful, but *to create new beauty.*" That was said by Wyndham Lewis, and it is surely addressed to the old schools and universities.

To lead a life sheltered from immediate ugliness and squalor in a mediæval cloister or Palladian quadrangle is not enough. Indeed it cannot be done. For one thing, it is obviously not a "life" at all. The attempt is constantly being made by sensitive people outside the Old Foundations in their private individual lives; and very difficult, costly and disappointing it almost invariably is.

With things as they are, the chief use of money to a person who is fastidious is to contrive a little private world of his own—an oasis of order, beauty and harmony in a dreary wilderness of hugger-mugger. So he builds or buys a beautiful house within a park shut off by a forbidding ring fence, and fills it with lovely things—books, pictures and furniture: he occasionally admits selected people of like mind to share his enjoyment of his treasures and to walk in his storm-girt Garden of Eden. It is all very cultivated and very civilised—if it were not for what lies outside the park. Also it is all immensely costly, cumbersome and artificial, and not nearly so satisfactory even to the owner as one might possibly expect.

You just cannot keep the world out. It insists

on breaking in every now and again, however thorough and complete your defences. Even if you only travel beyond your domain and your chosen neighbourhood well padded and blinkered, an occasional cold draught is sure to be let into your softly congenial orchid house by the most discreet of servants, visitors and correspondents, or by the newspapers, however carefully you select them.

It has therefore occurred to certain people that it would be a better idea to make the country generally safe for the fastidious to roam at large in, rather than to attempt or countenance this pill-box policy of isolated defence against what need not be.

It is an extremely expensive policy, absorbing a large proportion of the nation's wealth, it is only moderately effective, and there are those who would call it selfish. What is odd is that in these days we should tolerate such inefficiency—these immense efforts, these ludicrously small results—all for a tiny group of people who, quite rightly, want very much what we all want in the way of the Good Life and the peace and the leisure and the beauty thereof, but who have set about attaining their desires by means of this unwieldy piece of Heath Robinson mechanism—the Private Paradise.

The alternative is of course a world in which one could afford not to be rich, where paddings and blinkers and isolating mechanism would be unnecessary.

As things are, the Englishman who cares for beauty but who happens to be poor is likely to be perpetually affronted and to have a very thin time of it indeed. The odds being roughly a thousand to one on any one of us being below the economic beauty-line, this would not seem a very satisfactory state of things.

We talk glibly enough of the submerged tenth, too often forgetting that there are in addition eight-tenths or thereabouts who only manage with the greatest difficulty to keep their heads above pretty dirty water.

Certainly, unless you are really rich, it is wise to be born an Italian or a Scandinavian.

CHAPTER 9

THE GREAT HOUSE: ITS CONSERVATION AND CONVERSION

IT IS A FACT, PATENT TO ALL AND DEPLORED BY some, that the large-scale private paradise is already obsolescent. There are even now more great country houses in England than there are rich men able and willing to inhabit them. Even granted the large means necessary for their adequate staffing and upkeep, there are an increasing number of people who prefer supreme personal comfort, urban luxury, and mobile affluence free from all quasi-feudal ties and claims, to the formal state, local consequence and territorial responsibility implied by a large country place.

There are yet others who, having some sense of humour and proportion and a modern outlook, deliberately abdicate from a position that they find uncongenial and slightly ridiculous. They, too, have more amusing and often better uses for their time, energies and money than the maintenance of a great establishment—the stoking and oiling of a monstrous contrivance that, consuming and grinding through the years, produces—what?

Yet it is unthinkable that the great houses of England should be allowed to perish away—the really great houses, that is—those that are great in their architecture, their associations and the beauty of their settings, and not merely great in size. Size, indeed, has nothing to do with their claim to be preserved: it is quality, not bulk, that has survival value, as the unintelligent brontosaurus found to its cost.

We need to differentiate between the honest-to-God Stately Homes of England and the considerable tail of merely large or pretentious houses with no better claim to the title than an auctioneer's say-so. Auctioneers and estate agents have sanguine and obliging natures, and a professional pride that makes them scorn the mere architectural facts that might cripple or spoil their succulent " particulars."

It would be well if some impartial, authoritative and really critical commission could sit on our Country Seats and make a list of those which really deserve protection as national monuments and as characteristic and precious parts of England.

One could imagine the Editor of *Country Life* being asked to submit a draft list as a basis of discussion: his archives must surely contain authentic particulars and photographs of pretty nearly every house of real distinction in the land. That list would no doubt be modified by the inspection and findings of a grand inquisition that would present its regional reports.

We should then have to determine how many, and which, of the places recommended for preservation it would really be practicable to schedule as "untouchable." There would clearly be a limit to the number, and some system of rationing would be essential. In certain Welsh counties, for instance, the standard would need to be lowered a little, or else they might find themselves with no house at all that was dignified by State protection and assured to them as an adornment in perpetuity.

Wales and the Highlands of Scotland would, of course, be handsomely compensated by a richer collection of protected natural scenery; for, needless to say, statutory safeguarding would not be restricted merely to the works of man.

Whereas Northamptonshire might have a score of "protected" houses, the architecturally poor county would probably have a quota of but two or three, and those of a smaller and less noble kind.

There would be no attempt to spread the mantle of immunity evenly over the country, the idea being rather that, so far as was possible, no large area should be denied its permanent landmark of distinguished domestic architecture, and that no really notable building should be left at the mercy of mere utilitarianism or private caprice. Immunity would mean immunity not merely from unauthorised alteration, but from certain burdens. The scheduled house would enjoy substantial remissions from rates and taxes: it would carry very definite privileges with it as well as obligations.

The chief obligations would be to maintain the fabric of the house and such part of its surrounding demesne as might be scheduled with it in an adequate and conservative fashion; to submit to authority on all questions of major alterations; and to grant the public certain statutory privileges of access under carefully framed conditions.

The time is apparently coming when we can no longer look to unaided private piety for the upkeep and safeguarding of what are or should be our national heirlooms. The changes and chances of these unstable and swift-moving times are unfavourable to the *ancien régime* and the great memorials of that order; and many a fine old house has already suffered grievously either through the crippling poverty of its traditional owners or the prodigality of some new-rich carpet-bagger.

On the whole, however, we have now come to treat our architecturally important country houses with a due respect, and indeed the last few decades have seen a large amount of intelligent " rescue work " and sympathetic rehabilitation. It is probably the means for conservation that will be lacking, rather than the will or the requisite knowledge.

Needless to say, any worthy owner of a scheduled house would be given all possible inducements to continue as its occupier and guardian, and be enabled to transmit it to his issue by the operation of specially modified death duties.

Quite apart from any other consideration, an old house that is actually lived in by its traditional family or by a thoroughly understanding owner has unquestionably a bloom upon it and a human interest that the same place under purely official guardianship must definitely lack.

If and when a scheduled place was sold, the new purchaser would buy it subject to the various obligations and privileges legally attached to it, which would have been made to balance each other as justly as possible.

Certain heirlooms are already freed from death duties, and parks or other lands that have been formally and legally dedicated as permanent " open spaces " pay the duty at a reduced rate in proportion to the diminution in prospective building or other value that such dedication may entail. Savernake Forest, which though privately owned is publicly enjoyed, is a case in point.

In such ways the commissioners would strive to take the financial sting out of any restrictive covenants imposed upon a property. The effect on the national revenue would be trivial when compared with the widespread gain to national amenity both present and prospective.

One hears and one reads a good deal of sentimental gush about the heart-break of old-established landowners forced to sell their ancestral acres through the hardness of the times. Not infrequently, however, they are in low water through their own folly or mismanagement, or they have expensive tastes incompatible with the low returns from landowning. Briefly, though they may be attached to their inheritance, there are other things they care for more—it may be with good reason.

The most genealogically and antiquarian minded of us would scarcely quarrel even with a fifteenth earl for selling his historic seat rather than stint the education of his offspring. The cynical indifference, however, with which too many vendors seem to regard the ultimate fate of what they sell, cannot but make one a little suspicious of their auction-room anguish. They take no effective steps to prevent the instant desecration of their ancestral groves and meadows by mean buildings, the ruthless destruction of all the amenity that generations have created and guarded, or even of the mansion house itself.

Having themselves cleared out, they just let the whole place and its neighbourhood go hang.

No doubt the imposition of safeguarding clauses and covenants would reduce the price obtainable where the buyer's intention was to " break up " and " develop " an estate; but the landowner who sells out and clears out must choose between the extra cash and sympathy—he cannot have both.

Also there are no doubt certain legal difficulties

about making restrictive covenants effectively binding where no property is retained adjoining the freehold disposed of. There are, however, such things as 999-year leases whereby control can be retained, and there is always the alternative of the landowner personally co-operating in the development scheme and so guiding it aright, or of exploiting his land himself, to the best advantage, not merely to his privy purse but also in the cause of amenity, public as well as private.

The author has successfully practised what he here preaches, both in the way of protective covenants and as an owner-developer.

If—with expert assistance—landowners can sometimes farm their own land with pleasure and even profit, might they not more often attempt the analogous venture of building development, likewise under wise tutelage? Not infrequently a landowner unwilling to part with his old home nevertheless sells off the outlying parts of his estate, sometimes, with childish trustfulness, even up to his park palings. A few years on, and he finds himself hemmed in and beleaguered by a ragged belt of perky little houses that utterly destroy the amenity and value of what he had reserved. If he is as sensitive as he was foolish it will not be long before he himself slinks away, leaving the disease he allowed to gain a foothold to creep onward and inwards, until the heart itself of what had been a harmony of beauty is at last involved in the general ruin.

There are many estates having no claim to

" schedule " rank where the existing house and outworks would make an ideal nucleus for a new and " intentional " village. It seems clear from every point of view that new housing is better, more economically and more acceptably provided in sociable village units rather than as solitary individuals dotted sporadically about the country; and where the carefully chosen and well-matured site of an old country house can be secured for the founding of a new community, not only is there every chance of instantly securing both charm and individuality for what might else lack both for years or for ever, but also much of the initial spade-work of development will be found already done.

There are probably well-graded drives for approaches and communications, adequate water supply, drainage and sewage disposal arrangements, and most likely an electric lighting plant. The school, institute, clinic, church, club, cinema, stores, and whatever other accommodation be communally needed could probably be contrived within the fabric of the old house and outbuildings, as also no doubt laundry and bakehouse, or even a central kitchen if such be desired, possibly in conjunction with a communal dining-hall.

How pleasantly an ample stable court could be transformed into the central square—the surrounding buildings converted into shops and cottages, the turret clock chiming the hours no longer merely to grooms and chauffeurs, but to a new and more productive human society assembled there with the conscious purpose of civilised living. The rose-brick walls of the kitchen gardens now neatly enclose the village allotments, the ranges of glasshouses are in the profitable occupation of a tomato-grower, a goat farmer tenants the old kennels, a cabinet-maker has taken over the estate saw-mills, and a poultry farmer rents the one-time pheasantry.

Groups of new cottages are pleasantly disposed between the beech clumps and cedars on the old lawns, the most outlying abutting on the ha-ha that divides the garden from the park. Beyond that little gulf no building is allowed, the park having been dedicated as a permanent open space, let out as grazing to the new small-holder commoners where not reserved for playing-fields and tennis courts.

The new village is full of flowers and comely trees: it lies compact within a park and is approached by gracious avenues. Within a few years of its inception, such a settlement, skilfully planned, might well make a bid for that title that can never be awarded—" The Loveliest Village in England."

Perhaps someone of vision and enterprise who truly cares for his old home and yet must needs resign it as a private house, will thus forestall the speculator and demolition contractor and develop his property himself, wisely and decently, thereby not only avoiding offence to his ancestors, his neighbours, and the orderly-minded generally, but also providing himself with an absorbing and rewarding job.

Many great houses have, as it were, already insured their lives—some at a ripe old age—by taking up public work which may also save their souls. The author has had the privilege of transforming Stowe—a vast palace of some four hundred rooms—into a school, certain other houses into hotels, and one into a club.

Hospitals, homes of rest, asylums, summer schools, Civil Service and business-house staff clubs have likewise all found acceptable accommodation in *ci-devant* country houses, and if we say that we have no jobs for these we deceive ourselves.

Of course the candidates for public service need carefully selecting with special regard to their size, planning, construction and (which is where most will fail to qualify) their location. Undoubtedly there will be a certain number of dullish, unscheduled, ill-planned or ill-built large houses in out-of-the-way or uninteresting situations that will wither away because there is no particular reason (as with human unemployables) why they should survive or be preserved. But with so many reputable careers now open to them in the public service, in business, or as village nuclei, the big houses that are worth bothering about should rarely find it impossible to support themselves decently and with honour.

One assumes that conversion and conservation would be under the expert and sympathetic care of a competent architect, and that the amenities of the surroundings would be duly protected by a watchful management. Otherwise, what abominations and desolations, what indignities and disfigurements might not be perpetrated on some urbane old place by ignorant enthusiasts let loose on it, making the house wish that it had never been built, the garden and park that they had never been planted!

There is nothing so bitterly poignant to the amenity-minded as the sight of ancient loveliness being stupidly and unnecessarily ravaged. The loveliness of an ensemble such as we are considering can only be produced after generations of loving care and an immense expenditure of skilful labour; and its wanton destroyers must surely be as defective as those criminals who make unprovoked assaults upon their fellows, and should be quite as forcibly discouraged.

CHAPTER 10

THE BENEFICENT BUSYBODIES

THE REFORMS THUS FAR ADVOCATED AMOUNT to little more than this, then: adequate education and the co-operation of the privileged.

Obviously the new world must needs be chiefly made by new people, and the new people are made—well or ill—in the schools.

The raw material is all right (acquired characteristics being mercifully uninheritable): so if we want better sausages we must overhaul and improve the machine.

Civilised children will become civilised citizens: we should then get civilised central and local government produced by a more exacting public opinion, and—ultimately—a really civilised country.

And meanwhile, what is the private individual to do to bring nearer that still distant consummation?

First, he will use his eyes, he will read and he will think, and he will draw certain deductions, some of them correct. He will sift his impressions and think again, and discuss and persuade and be persuaded. He (and of course she) will vote and speak, and perhaps write, on what seems to be the side of the angels. To those who, in our sense, behave themselves unseemly, he will be valiantly rude or sorrowfully reproachful as will in the circumstances be most effective.

Those who do the right thing, whether by accident or design, he will praise unstintedly, making known their good deeds in a naughty world as loudly and widely as he possibly can, so that their neighbours shall marvel and say, " It seems that Jones is a remarkably fine fellow—he has put up what they call ' Good Lettering ' over his shop—he has scraped the advertisements off his garage front—he has got the railway to plant trees round the station yard, and has had his new villa designed by a real architect—all of which appears to have made him prominent, popular and happy: let us too look into this amenity stuff and see if there isn't something in it."

Examples of such minor amelioration will occur to the observant. Leicester, for instance, has shown us how far that little detail, good commercial lettering, can go towards the redeeming of a town not otherwise distinguished: from Arundel the cult for well-painted inn signs has spread all over Sussex, to the great gain of its villages: Carnarvonshire is wisely reverting to the use of whitewash—its simple buildings thereby recapturing much of their traditional charm.

The cause's well-wisher will also acquaint himself with the existing law and make the necessary fuss if his county, borough or district council has not availed itself of the right to make helpful by-laws or, having made them, fails to enforce them.

In certain counties, for instance, the provisions of the Rural Workers' Housing Act of 1926 have been made inoperative by the inaction of the councils.

Has a town-planning scheme been adopted, and is it being wisely put into force ? Are there proper by-laws against disfigurement by advertisements or the pollution of streams, or in furtherance of coal-smoke abatement ? If so, are they really operative, or become a dead letter ? Are all the members of the council disinterested and well-intentioned, and are the inspector and surveyor enlightened, competent and sympathetic, or would a little pointed criticism be wholesome ?

One way and another there is a lot that a beneficent busybody can do, and there are a number of increasingly powerful societies to support him.

Happily, too, there is now a general clearing-house in the recently formed Council for the Preservation of Rural England, or " C.P.R.E.,"[1] and any complaint, report, suggestion or question addressed to it is either dealt with direct or sent on to the appropriate society or authority.

Needless to say, the good busybody will not

[1] 33, Bloomsbury Square, W.C. 1.

plunge ignorantly into criticism and meddling without preparation, but will take the trouble necessary to discover what are the qualities to be looked for in a building, the presence of which will elevate it into the realm of architecture. The great mass of everyday modern building (in England) is, of course, not architecture at all, not because it is small or plain, but because it lacks all sense of coherence, proportion, mass and line, and because the materials are ill-chosen or improperly used.

Decent architecture does not mean any greater expenditure of money—only of thought and skill.

The " beginner " might find some such catechism as the following helpful in determining whether any particular building is in a state of grace or no.

1. Are you practical—that is, are you an efficient house, shop, school, factory or church? Can a family be brought up in you, or cheese be sold, or children taught, or boots made, or services be conducted in you with convenience?

2. Are you soundly and honestly built and lastingly weatherproof?

3. If you are new, are you going to look (*a*) shabby or (*b*) still raw, in ten years time, or have your materials been so wisely chosen and employed that the years will pleasantly mature and mellow you?

4. Are you beautiful, or at any rate to me, or if not, did you seem so to those who built you, and if so, why?

5. Do you express some sort of an idea—are you, for instance, notably restful or vigorous, emphatically horizontal or vertical, demure or gay, refined or robust, light or dark, feminine or masculine? Generally, have you "character," and if so, of what kind?

6. Are you a good neighbour—do you love the Georgian inn next door, or the Regency chemist's shop opposite, or the pollarded lime trees, or the adjoining church and elm grove, as yourself? Do you do-as-you-would-be-done-by? Do the other buildings and the hills and trees and your surroundings near you generally gain or lose by your presence? In short, have you civilised manners?

Those are the sort of questions that a building should be expected to answer—and *will* answer, readily and volubly, to a reasonably skilful examiner.

Such inquiries will naturally lead on to more detailed and technical analysis of a building's make-up.

What, for instance, is the proportion between wall surface and window openings, what the proportions of the windows themselves and even of their panes? Are they successful and pleasant, or is the effect either blank and depressing or distractingly fussy?

How is the roof treated? Does it finish behind a parapet or overhang at the eaves, and if so, too much or too little?

Is the pitch of the roof too high or too low or

just right—are its slates or tiles of pleasant colour and texture, soft and "strokeable," or crude, hard and machine-made-looking?

Are the chimneys tall and important enough, or, on the other hand, top-heavy-looking? If there are mouldings or stone dressings, are they well proportioned and well placed, or over-emphatic or overdone?

Finally, is it a decent, sensible, straightforward-looking job, or a brutal, mutton-fisted "Don't Care" botch, or a silly, dolled-up affair of whim-whams and features that make it a worse neighbour than the downright "tough"—the frankly blackguard building that has no pretences or illusions about being genteel?

To be able to size up and classify and condemn or approve every building that you come across—as you may soon come to do instinctively—naturally adds prodigiously to the interest of your surroundings, wherever you may be, at home or abroad.

That it adds pain as well as pleasure goes without saying, but it is only through such suffering that the good citizen is brought to birth. He will, of course, aid and expedite his own delivery and subsequent growth to usefulness by reading and discussion, but above all by using and training his eyes.

Having acquired the habit of observation and analysis and a reasonably sure taste, then let him prophesy and proselytise and do something for England.

In Russia there are three hundred thousand more or less self-appointed critics of things in general, who send in periodic grumbles or commendations or suggestions to a central bureau, which brings them to the notice of the appropriate authorities and publishes the more important of them in semi-official journals. These citizen-correspondents have a privileged position, and appear to make the most of it by maintaining a hot fire of constructive criticism that keeps headquarters in a perpetual fizz of activity. That's the kind of thing we want over here—local correspondents all over the country, with watching briefs from G.H.Q., constantly on the alert and reporting everything affecting the amenities of their particular localities for good or ill.

We ought never to be taken by surprise—we want to know where milk is likely to be spilt and be beforehand with helpful advice or preventive protest instead of feebly crying after the event. We want to replace subsequent lamentations by a sufficiently early " We'll be damned if you shall ! "

Most people, we must remember, are neither with us nor against us, merely from lack of imagination or lack of thought or observation, and their indifference and inertia we must try to overcome by educative propaganda.

This great majority—the unburied dead—are a perpetual drag on all progress whatsoever. Others there are who cynically confess that they have no interest in the preservation of anything, and are ready to exploit and desecrate hill and valley, waterfall and seaboard to any extent and without shame if only they can extract a money profit from the venture.

Being clearly defective in their social consciences, such people must be forcibly restrained from their depredations by adequate legal safeguards.

A number of specific cases come to mind substantiating this indictment, and it would be a real pleasure to publish the names and addresses of the malefactors—a pleasure, however, that the existing law of libel makes prohibitively costly. This admirable service, however, is warmly commended to the notice of some public-spirited millionaire, pugnacious and litigious enough to enjoy the necessary rumpus and rich enough to bear the costs when judgment went against him. He would be doing heroic work for his defenceless country, and earning the undying gratitude of his own and all future generations.

The one difficulty is that millionaires are not like that—they are preternaturally timid, and they are themselves amongst the worst offenders. South Wales has suffered many things because of them—ravishings, mutilations, and indignities that the utmost penitential service could not wipe out.

Any stand however valiant against the development or exploitation of natural resources or against legitimate industry of any kind is foredoomed to failure—probably rightly. Times are hard, competition is fierce, and the earth (so we hold in our complacency) was made for man.

For man, for *every man*, not only or chiefly for company promoters and speculators.

There is a certain exquisitely lovely Welsh valley of grey crags and tumbling water that must have entranced all who have passed that way from time immemorial. Now the baleful eye of an alien financier has lit upon it and seen that it is good—for the promotion of a company.

He is going to blast the rocks for minerals, imprison the waterfall in a pipe for power, and choke the flowery valley bottom with a slum of miners' barracks.

Competent and disinterested technicians have reported that there is scarcely a hope of the enterprise paying, but it matters little to the promoter whether it does or not. It all makes very enticing reading in his prospectus, and the concession being conveniently remote, the subscribers are unlikely ever to come and inspect the proposition for themselves. If they did, they would find not dissimilar undertakings bankrupt and abandoned, ominously dotted about the neighbourhood in a way that might well give them pause.

What has been the net result of all these abortive ravishings? The face of the country has been irreparably disfigured, a great many foolish and relatively innocent people have wasted and lost a great deal of money—most of which has gone in making a horrible mess, but some to the enriching of the kind of persons we should hate to be seen talking to.

From the point of view of the commonweal it is not an encouraging sort of balance-sheet. Even if there be actual money profit for a time, the loss is everlasting. But company promoters and concession hunters and those who finance them seem to be without bowels, incorrigible. None but deaf adders, surely, could resist the eloquence of that mighty charmer, Ruskin?

> "The sun had drawn landscapes for you . . . in green and blue and all imaginable colours, here in England. Not one of you ever looked at them then; not one of you cares for the loss of them now, when you have shut the sun out with smoke. There was a rocky valley between Buxton and Bakewell, once upon a time, divine as the vale of Tempe; you might have seen the gods there morning and evening—Apollo and all the sweet Muses of the Light, walking in fair procession on the lawns of it, and to and fro among the pinnacles of its crags. You cared neither for gods nor grass but for cash (which you did not know the way to get). You thought you could get it by what *The Times* calls 'Railroad Enterprise.' You enterprised a railroad through the valley, you blasted its rocks away, heaped thousands of tons of shale into its lovely stream. The valley is gone, and the gods

with it; and now every fool in Buxton can be at Bakewell in half an hour and every fool in Bakewell in Buxton; which you think a lucrative process of exchange, you Fools, everywhere!"[1]

That was written in 1871, nearly two generations ago; and what good has it done? What good can any writing do? Something, perhaps, but not much.

If a Government has one function above all others, surely it is to protect the natural heritage and rights of its future citizens against the infringements of selfish squanderers in our present time.

Should these disfiguring operations be permitted unless there is some reasonable assurance that they are going to justify themselves by success, and should not those performing them be held responsible for tidying up such mess as they have made within a reasonable time of their activities coming to an end? Civilised children should put away their toys when their game is over.

It might be a little harsh to ask mine-owners to shovel their spoil heaps back down their pits when their mines closed down, much as we might like to, but we might very reasonably require them to restore the face of nature so far as was practicable by sowing and planting, and by the demolition of their derelict buildings.

[1] *Fors Clavigera.*

It will doubtless be pointed out that though such undertakings may flourish for years and make large profits for their owners, the very fact of their closing down is often the result of bankruptcy, either through the exhaustion of the minerals worked or through adverse trade conditions or mismanagement. In such circumstances there will clearly be no funds forthcoming for a valedictory clean-up.

That is very true, and to get over this difficulty it is suggested that every industrial concern whose activities are held by the competent authority to affect amenities adversely, shall be required to establish a special reserve fund or to deposit an adequate sum with the said authority as stakeholder, as a surety and guarantee that they will be able (if not willing) to leave things decently and in order. Unless the abandoned buildings were so designed as to be readily convertible to some other use, or chanced to be architecturally and picturesquely acceptable as ruins (as the ruins of a castle are acceptable), complete demolition might be required.

In Cornwall the gaunt chimneys and pumping-houses of the worked-out tin mines are often rather an adornment than otherwise to the bleak and rather forlorn-looking landscape to which they seem the fitting climax.

A thorough tree-planting scheme would be adopted and put in hand for the clothing of any scars in the earth itself wherever possible, and any housing that became redundant through the cessation of a local industry would be demolished, the components being removed to wherever they might profitably be re-used for new construction.

As the stake required to be deposited against the clean-up would be assessed according to the prospective difficulty, extent, and cost of that restitution, those who made the least mess or who tidied up as they went along would get off much more lightly than a concern which surrounded itself with unsightly squalor in the bad old way. The guarantee fund would put a premium on ordered neatness and circumspection and would certainly be a serious deterrent to the gambling prospector and company promoter, though, as the calls for the contributions to the fund would only be made periodically and according to the development of the enterprise, and as the bank interest on the deposit would go to the depositor, it should not bear harshly on legitimate business of reasonably assured prospects.

If the levy were to be based on the profits held out in the prospectuses of new issues, it might soon rival the road fund, or, alternatively, constrain the not disinterested enthusiasts who prepare such documents, to some regard for probability.

At present most of our industrialists are even more anti-social than Cockney picnickers or than the tramps who cast their worn-out boots and clothing by the wayside. They have no manners. Speculative builders are as bad—demolition is the only sure cure for most of their crimes, but that again is a remedy too drastic to receive much support.

There is indeed an enlightened municipality that, on a vote of the ratepayers, condemns and demolishes the town's most unworthy building every year, but that, needless to say, is not in the British Isles. For one thing, British ratepayers would almost certainly vote the wrong ticket—if they troubled to vote at all.

This is the Country of the Blind—we cannot see and we do not care.

We are told that the old sectarian religions wear thin. Is there not a religion of beauty and fitness, of efficiency and fair play, that should wake a quick response in modern humanity if patiently and sympathetically presented?

The Council for the Preservation of Rural England is but a special missionary in that great field, working steadily, persistently and above all tactfully towards beauty and the appreciation of beauty—not hastily nor vociferously in any revivalist frenzy.

Like the League of Nations, it must have authority if it is to carry out its beneficent mission —it must enlist the people of light and leading in its support, both men and women, especially such fortunate persons as are in such a position that they can prove their faith by works. Landlords, industrialists, journalists, municipalities, district councillors, architects, surveyors, contractors, and all those having any control of public or private works of any sort, should be eager to make manifest their soundness of heart by giving the Council, or some constituent local or special society, their practical support.

They *should* be—but will they be? Perhaps England is in sober truth one of the " Backward Peoples." We shall see.

CHAPTER XI

PROPAGANDA, POLITICS AND PRESS

IT IS QUITE POSSIBLE, PERHAPS PROBABLE, THAT there will be a great reaction and revulsion against the doings and omissions of the last few generations, and that we or our children, having regained consciousness, will view with consternation the wreckage wrought in our delirium.

We shall say, " Good God ! What *have* we done —what have we *not* done—what now . . . ? "

Whilst we just begin to stir uneasily towards a normal sanity, and only a few of us at that, the nightmare horror goes on and on unceasingly, increasingly, catastrophically. For every year of doing now there will be a generation of undoing and expiation, and many of the evil things will remain with us for ever.

At present we are so foolishly defenceless against outrage of any and every sort from whatever cause or quarter threatened, as a rule indeed not even hearing that some new calamity is upon us until it is an accomplished and blistering fact. Even if we do get fair warning of dirty work ahead, usually all we can do is to set up yet another dismal howl of protest that irritates and depresses but seldom accomplishes anything.

Often the doer of the ill deed will plead economic necessity: the Borough Council will say it must pull down the almshouses to make room for the trams, the speculator will say bungalows pay and trees don't.

Freehold property is at present almost as unreservedly yours to do as you please with as is your waistcoat or your watch. There is no legal compulsion on you to use it in a way that will be acceptable and inoffensive to your neighbours and the general public. If what you propose to do outrages them, their only remedy is to bribe you from your purpose by purchase or cajolery, or scare you from it by public protests—which is an extremely unsatisfactory state of things.

Never having troubled to protect ourselves as a community or our country as a whole by reasonable safe-guarding laws, because we could think of nothing but private rights and private property (which we protected inordinately), we have no efficient or scientific machinery wherewith to cope with infringements against our natural liberties.

Indeed there is no effective machinery whatever, and each new emergency is faced in a state of planless panic, and we bleat and blether and appeal until someone is moved to come to the rescue with so many hundreds or thousands of pounds, or, more often, the blackmail not being forthcoming, the abhorred thing is done despite our wringing of hands.

As the Government is apt to shirk responsibility just where it and it alone could assure orderly development, reasonable conservation and general fair dealing—in short as it mostly abrogates what ought to be one of its chief functions—the altruistic minority that cares what becomes of England has to spend its time and its money in attempts, mostly futile, to mitigate the disastrous effects of public and official negligence.

It is really one of our morbid symptoms that if any place of natural beauty or historic interest is to be sold, we forthwith attempt to raise a fund for its purchase for the nation.

It is called "saving it"—why? Because we know well that if it is not so bought it will almost certainly be built over, desecrated and destroyed. We have indeed almost become a museum in which are preserved here and there carefully selected and ticketed specimens of what England *was*. The National Trust is England's executor.

If any private estate were managed anything like as inefficiently as England is mishandled and maladministered as a whole, there would be no difficulty whatever in getting the proprietor locked up as a dangerous lunatic. As it is, our land-tenure and certain other laws are manifestly so grotesquely inadequate for the protection of public amenity and the natural resources of our country that they must certainly be altered, and quite profoundly.

Can we by any means get them so altered in our own time, or are we to suffer the increasingly rapid dissipation of our remaining assets for yet another generation?

A supine Government and the persistence of laws that tolerate the irresponsible and purely self-regarding owning and use of land are merely reflections of our futile, muddle-headed selves; and we have only sufficiently to desire and deserve better things to get them.

The time has come for those who care about amenity to hitch their wagon to a political policy, if not indeed to a party. A careful and authoritative report should be forthwith prepared, comparable with the Liberal Brown Book Report, and it would be discovered from which of the existing parties helpful legislation was most likely to be forthcoming.

Those who have ever given election-time help at committee-rooms will recall the miscellaneous sort of pressure to which a candidate is subjected. Both the temperance party and the brewing interest wish to be positively assured of his soundness on the liquor question: others interested, it may be, in Prayer-book reform or in farming wish to know whether he favours the use of the chasuble in the first case or a bounty on sugar beet in the second.

Now is there not something to be learnt from these importunate people? Many of them will be cranks and axe-grinding self-seekers, but there is something to be said for their methods.

It is the general assumption that the laws of this country, besides discouraging certain violent sorts of wrongdoing and controlling our conduct in a variety of ways, also set up by implication a certain standard of morality.

Supposing there were two sorts of naughtiness (" Torts," or whatever they may be), for the doing of which you were normally fined ten shillings and forty shillings respectively. There would certainly grow up in the public mind a very definite idea that it must be roughly four times as wicked to commit the second offence as to commit the first.

In the same naïve way our legislators undoubtedly gauge the relative importance of political questions, both local and imperial, by the amount of fuss their constituents make about them at election time, whilst the public in turn forms its notions of priority from the prominence given to various subjects in politics and consequently in the Press.

Now if we could get questions of amenity into the brilliantly lit field between these two reflecting mirrors, we should have done the greatest thing immediately possible for the preservation of England. We should have made the things we care about seem important—even worth quarrelling and voting about—which is perhaps as much as is possible in a democratic country.

Which party will stand forth as the avowed champion of a more civilised way of life and of a better, more orderly and more beautiful world, by giving amenity and the visual arts their due place in its programme ?

Once it was realised that such matters were actual politics—that something might be done about them—the candidate who took them seriously and in a reforming spirit would find a new and by no means despicable suffrage at his command.

This applies, of course, not merely to parliamentary candidates, but to those for municipal, county and local councils also.

To begin with, at any rate, it will not be much use demanding to know a candidate's views on amenity questions—he won't have any. It will be the duty of the intelligent and zealous voter to supply him with a good reliable set, and then to see that he is actively faithful to them in his constituency and in the House.

After all, a great deal of building and other work in the country is in some way or another under the control either of Parliament or of the municipal or other local authorities. Why cannot the right-minded, whether their views be Conservative, Liberal or Labour, go to their respective candidates, whether for Parliament, County Council, or whatever, and offer to work for them and vote for them if in their turn they will at least promise not to vote without protest for any project architecturally or æsthetically unworthy ? They must promise, for instance, that if they get on the County Council and a new school or hospital is to be built, they will endeavour to see that a proper competition is instituted, or that some competent architectural authority is consulted. Or, again, they could see that some little word shall be slipped into this or that Bill or public regulation which would make for beauty instead of for ugliness. Why should the County Council's new bridge be permitted to look like an orphan pauper when, with a little skill, it might so easily be transformed into a princess?

To your candidate all this will probably be a matter of entire indifference, and in exchange for your help he will willingly promise to act in a matter where, alas, feeling can hardly be said to run high.

At all of which there will be snorts of indignation. " Would you then lower the greatest of the arts to struggle in the political arena? Would you allow the ' Mistress Art ' to cover herself with the dust of conflict and descend to party politics?"

The reply is, of course, " Most certainly!" Architecture has stood aloof far too long. In the great epochs of architecture when people really talked about it and knew about it and practised it, then the " Mistress Art " frequented not only the party arena but the back stairs, and did not disdain the protection of ladies like Nell Gwynne.

No good can come of architects who sky themselves like Nelson on his isolating pedestal, or try to keep Madame Architecture mewed up in the drawing-room like the " Godly Matron " of the Victorians.

Architects cannot even bring themselves to write

frank and bitter criticisms of each other's works as authors can and do, greatly to the invigoration of their art and of the public. They cannot meddle with politics: they will not sully themselves with this, that, or the other.

Look back: such squeamish fastidiousness was never the hall-mark of the great period of any art. Granted, there is the difficulty of the artistic temperament; but it can only be indulged beyond a certain point at the expense of the individual's own character both as an artist and a citizen, and of the commonweal.

The good architects merely look askance at the outrages or infelicities perpetrated by their weaker brethren, and pass by on the other side with a shudder; but the good architect who was also a good citizen would surely work and pray for the segregation or extermination of the incompetent.

Trades unionism is not enough. . . . True, architectural education within the profession was never in better case, and the various architectural schools are now turning out hundreds of young men and women each year, soundly instructed and thoroughly imbued with the principles of right building.

There are probably already enough perfectly competent architects, young, middle-aged and old, to plan and supervise all the building now being done or likely to be done throughout the country. We have educated a noble army of architects, but we have neglected to educate the building public up to employing them.

A painter can paint his canvases front and back and many times over and exercise his talent to a large extent without a patron or a public at a trivial cost to himself; a poet can bring his most ambitious works to birth, if not to publication, at the cost of a few pence for ink and paper; but an architect must find a mother for his child—someone to bear the burden of realising the designer's scheme—to body it forth, as it were, in flesh and blood.

An architect can do little fruitful planning in the abstract; he needs a definite problem setting for solution—the essence of a successful design being that it takes into consideration all the conditions and peculiarities of site, function, materials and client, and by analysis, synthesis and skilful compromise contrives to meet the conditions imposed in a direct, economical and pleasing fashion.

No, even spiritually, an architect cannot live by drawing alone, which is indeed no more than an incidental process in his real work of getting great masses of material in bewildering variety disposed solidly and harmoniously upon the earth in obedience to his will.

It is fascinating, often intoxicating work, and, as architecture is an art and a vocation and not merely a profession, it will be found that all true architects are conspicuous for the tirelessness and gusto with which they do what it is their delight to do. And yet, whilst on the one hand there are tens of thousands of inefficient and altogether deplorable houses going up all over the country that are not within a hundred miles of being architecture of any sort, there are, on the other hand, hundreds of young architects unemployed or under-employed.

At present not one in a thousand of the new villas and bungalows have the unmistakable and honourable stigmata of legitimacy—the clean and simple lines and sound constitution that proclaim a building born in wedlock of an architect. How graciously the one stands forth in its quiet dignity from the bastard brood: what a relief is its reticence amidst the silly monkey-chatter of the half-wits— so misshapen, so tawdry, so rickety, so generally defective and pathetic.

Are we doing anything really effective to remedy this crazy state of things? Are the architects themselves making adequate efforts to educate the public, to create that demand for decent architecture without which demand it obviously cannot prevail?

The Architecture Club was founded to this end and has, with its exhibitions of photographs and its Press committee, certainly done something. Mr. J. C. Squire, the Club's president, wields a valiant pen, but the Press generally is even now but half awakened.

We must remember, however, that the ordinary newspaper will only supply an existing demand— it will do little to create one, that is, if the demand be for something rather abstract and fundamental and permanent, and not a mere flash in the pan to be "featured" violently for a week or so and then dropped for some new thing.

That demand must be made by the public at the instigation of the propagandist, who will have his work cut out for him.

CHAPTER XII

SURSUM CORDA

It may be held that the picture of contemporary England sketched out in the foregoing chapters is unwarrantably gloomy, and that things are not yet as bad as all that. The reader may gratefully recall certain stretches of lovely and unspoiled country where he has perhaps walked for the best part of a summer's day without affront—or some remote old village where, if the breath of change has not entirely passed it by, has at any rate not blasted.

There are, thank God, still many such exceptions to the general rule of devastation—just enough to make our strivings to defend what is left to us worth while. No more. Had things gone much further one could scarcely have made out a convincing case for an effort to save the amenities of England: one would have been asked blankly what there was to save, and even been put to it to produce typical examples of what was still worthy of protection.

But conservation of what there is will not be nearly enough, even if it were thorough and complete from this day forth for evermore, which it will certainly not be.

Broadly speaking, we may hope—not that the mess will not be added to—but that the annual "mess-rate" will be progressively diminished until ultimately, perhaps, it reaches vanishing point, as it has in Sweden and certain other civilised States.

Not even then, however, shall we be able to hold up our heads in such company unless we have not merely *done* creditably from now on but also *un*done concurrently on a quite heroic scale. We have been the world's most miserable sinners for a century past, and until quite recently there was no health in us—not enough, at any rate, to combat the disease.

Mercifully, and perhaps just in time, there is now a small minority fully, even passionately alive to our misdeeds both past and present, and determined that, so far as in them lies, England shall cease to grow less lovely year by year, but shall halt, then face about, and begin to regain order and beauty. Not necessarily, indeed not possibly, the beauty of the eighteenth or seventeenth or any other century, but a new beauty from a new and intelligent synthesis of needs and factors that are utterly different from any in the past.

Let us examine the scattered evidences of returning health and sanity, and then the changed conditions that are even now changing and that must and will change England itself for decades to come—for better or for worse, according to our will.

It is not that there was no light to lighten the darkness—Cobbett and Wordsworth, Ruskin and Morris, were the linkmen of England's darkest century; but their benighted and preoccupied countrymen apprehended them not, or merely cried one to another, " Oh! what a pretty light!" and neither followed it nor worked by its radiance. Or if they did follow, they went astray and got utterly lost, as did those, for instance, who were led by the beguiling *ignis fatuus* of John Ruskin's *Seven Lamps of Architecture*.

They were brilliant lamps enough, but as practical guiding lights they were too dazzling, their beams darting hither and thither from the profound to the Most High, and not showing the plain man the path he was to tread. Largely it was the fault of the plain man, who was too plain, and who took his Ruskin—who was perhaps not plain enough—too literally, mistaking his poetic exhortations for a text-book's instructions.

It is one of the signs of our returning health that Ruskin is now being read critically and with large reservations and is becoming honoured as a social reformer and a champion of order and decency rather than as an arbiter of taste or a guide to right building.

But there are other signs and portents numerous enough and significant enough to make it possible —one cannot yet say probable—that the dawn is at hand. Midnight struck some time in the latter part of last century, perhaps as late as the 'nineties, and the day breaks very slowly—so slowly indeed that the watchers have wondered if the dawn would ever come.

But now there are bars and streaks of light such as have not been seen for generations: there are still dark banks of cloud, sullen and oppressive, but they are shot through and pierced with the morning light, and are no longer the unbroken masses that they were.

Knowledge, good-will and energy begin to be applied to our everyday works on a scale and in a way that has appreciable effects. But if many things are now being done both wisely and well, there are far, far more that are still done stupidly, meanly and shamefully.

That we must face, that too we must alter.

Amongst the hopeful signs we may certainly count the following that have already been referred to. The more intelligent of the general public have definitely begun to care about amenity. True, it is a small minority, but it is definitely there—so much there that even the daily Press has realised that there is a certain " News Value " in questions of preservation, in acts of vandalism threatened or accomplished, and in plans for new buildings or in town-planning proposals.

Likewise, the very Government has lately become conscious of this growing public opinion; and in spite of its belated awakening to its responsibility in these matters and its halting and perfunctory legislation, a certain official bias in favour of ordered towns and an unsullied country is already just perceptible.

That may not seem a very proud boast, but in view of the record of the administrations of the past hundred years it is really a prodigious advance. Indeed, thanks mainly to the initiative of certain enlightened and zealous high Civil servants, Government control or intervention has in many recent instances actually saved the situation, and the officially blessed scheme has been far better than a few years ago one would have dared to hope.

Within its far too limited powers, the Ministry of Health is now manifestly on the right side, and if its intentions in the matter of housing schemes were always interpreted by a competent architect on the spot, which unhappily they are not, one would have little to complain of in what has lately been done under this department.

Almost invariably an official state-aided housing scheme is a far more civilised affair in every way than an ordinary private enterprise building estate, in lay-out, in the character of the actual houses and in amenities generally. One could not say less than that—one might say a little more. Considering the wholesale nature of these undertakings, we have certainly come off a great deal better than we deserved, or had any right to expect under the circumstances. Had there been no new housing but Council housing since the War we had been in far happier case to-day, so far as the look of England is concerned.

Yet had the responsible Ministers cared for seemliness and taken adequate steps to ensure a modicum of architectural decency in the million houses they were bringing into being, what miles of tedious insipidity might we not have been spared! Neither the Addison Act nor the Wheatley Act so much as mentioned the word " amenity "; there was not so much as a distant gesture of salutation towards seemliness or good design; and the marvel is that somehow or other, here and there, the results were sometimes positively attractive.

Adjoining the old prison at Warwick is an admirable new colony: there is another at Winchescheester, and several in Berkshire. Hitchin, and, of course, Welwyn are both exemplary, Hertfordshire as a whole having indeed come off very well. Much praise may also be given to Chesterfield and Newark, though the north of England has not been more generally fortunate than has South Wales.

Buckinghamshire, Northamptonshire, Lancashire and Yorkshire are perhaps the counties that have been the least successful in their housing enterprises from an architectural and amenity point of view.

For the new village near Hendon and the later work at Becontree and elsewhere, the London County Council deserves our respectful thanks, whilst the excellent new post offices and telephone exchanges erected under the Office of Works show that department to be architecturally right-minded, as did the great concrete building at Acton run up after the War for the Ministry of Pensions.

Also shortly after the War the Ministry of Agriculture made a valiant gesture of recognition towards amenity and right building, more particularly as regards small holdings. That, however, may have been due to the individual initiative of the then responsible departmental head, Sir Lawrence Weaver—a stout and eloquent champion of the architectural decencies and of amenity generally.

Whether the multiplication of societies for the protection of this or prevention of that is more a sign of returning health or of an acceleration of disease it is perhaps difficult to judge.

One may at least say this : the ravages incidental to the malady are no longer being accepted fatalistically and as a matter of course, but arouse a growing chorus of protest and resentment.

The present need is for such protests to be made effective more quickly and more certainly, until such time as a new and wiser way of life may have made impossible the misdeeds that now provoke them.

A Devil's Dictionary

Containing Some Specific Complaints, Warnings, and Proposals

Advertisements

ADVERTISEMENTS ARE ONLY OFFENSIVE WHEN out of place. Newspapers, railway stations and urban hoardings are their proper habitat, and any advertiser who strays outside the generous accommodation so provided risks the alienation of the more enlightened public.

Roadside placards or other inacceptable displays certainly produce a very definite reaction *against* the goods it is sought to popularise, an established psychological phenomenon that the old-fashioned advertiser seems to have not yet discovered.

The more progressive tyre and petrol firms have realised this and have withdrawn all their advertisements throughout the country, to its very great gain and their own profit.

The worst offender at the present time is probably the Raleigh Cycle Company. One wonders why a company which manufactures a reliable type of cycle upon which thousands ride out from the towns to enjoy the country should persist in destroying the amenities of our roadsides by the erection of yellow advertisements which even the most phlegmatic among us cannot pass without a shock.

The way in which many of our larger towns have allowed their main approaches to be devastated by advertising is truly surprising. Some of them devote large sums to the maintenance of civic dignity at their centres, but leave their boundaries to be as tatterdemalion and slattern as they please.

London itself is particularly dishonoured by the vulgar babel along the Bath Road almost to Maidenhead. Shrewsbury, in many ways well-mannered, falls sadly from grace on the road out towards Wales, along which hotels and garages clamour for one's notice. The attention given is surely more frequently resentful than the hoardings' owners can imagine.

If garages and hotels could only arrange (perhaps under the auspices of the A.A.) to adopt appropriate, well-designed and standardised signs or symbols for roadside display, the motoring public would be spared much anguish and confusion, and the proprietors of such places much unnecessary expense. The form and colour of the conventional sign would at once proclaim what was being offered, whether garage, inn, teashop or what-not; the name would appear in good clear lettering on a tablet, the quality and standing of the establishment being impartially proclaimed by an appropriate number of stars—as in a guide-book.

Swift locomotion has really revived the need for the symbolism of the Middle Ages: the written word is becoming as indecipherable to the mile-a-minute motorist as it was to the twelfth-century villein.

That enterprising American journal, *Homes and Gardens*, has published a wide series of well-designed signs with this need in view—the need in that country being the more urgent partly because of the more frantic roadside touting. It is no uncommon thing for the clamour to begin a hundred miles away—" 100 miles to the Dewdrop Inn: Fried Chicken Lunches." " 99 miles to the Dewdrop Inn: Fried Chicken Lunches "—and so on down to one, and ultimately to the zero of that Via Dolorosa.

Even Japan has its advertising afflictions, as Sir Rabindranath Tagore's address to Japanese students makes painfully clear.

" Have you never felt shame when you see the trade advertisements, not only plastering the whole town with lies and exaggerations, but invading the green fields, where the peasants do their honest labour, and the hill-tops, which greet the first pure light of the morning ? . . . This commercialism with its barbarity of ugly decorations is a terrible menace to all humanity, because it is setting up the ideal of power over that of perfection."

In America advertising is quite literally in the air—the broadcasting of advertisements having become a regular part of the wireless service.

There are those who deplore this enterprising employment of the ether, and who call it a prostitution of science. Merciful science, however, has provided a means to the instant relief of any suffering through its most valuable invention, the cut-out switch, but there is as yet no such emergency exit from the importunities of the hoardings.

Aerodromes

In all probability we shall live to see a multiplication of air stations and landing grounds all over the British Isles in connection with civil aviation.

To some extent the new and cleanly planned air terminus at Croydon has corrected the bad example set by the military aerodromes; but it is to be hoped that the responsible authorities will not disdain to take their cue for the design of their new airport buildings from certain continental examples, particularly in Germany. They should not forget—they quite well may—that the appearance of their buildings from the air is at least as important as the traditional man's-eye view of them from the ground.

It is also to be hoped that some regard may be paid to pre-existing land-lubber amenities in the actual placing of aerodromes, and that the Stonehenge scandal will not be repeated. There, with all Salisbury Plain to choose from, the R.F.C. (as it then was) elected to plump down its hangars and all their sprawling appurtenances within a

the Octopus

few hundred yards of what should be the most hallowed stones in England. Never were venerable remains less venerated, for at this very moment of writing, our late enemies having declined our military invitation to obliterate the circle with their bombs, an offensive pink bungalow is being completed hard by that, with the outrageous café adjoining, makes one almost pray for a destructive air raid.

As it now is, Stonehenge is intolerable, and by no means to be visited save by blind archæologists. Hemmed in by iron railings, guarded by a turnstile and a post-card kiosk, glowered at by the derelict aerodrome and smirked at by café and bungalow, this sacred place is indeed painful beyond bearing. If it were an even chance that a hostile air raid would destroy the circle or, alternatively, obliterate the parasitic growths about it, there are probably those who would favour the place being well and truly bombed.

As it is, Stonehenge is a mockery and a wounding of the spirit, and a fifty-fifty risk of losing it altogether or getting it back once more in its austere and immemorial loneliness might well seem a gamble worth considering.

Archæologists and Antiquaries

THESE, like elephants, are generally useful but sometimes extremely dangerous. Their gimlet eyes have a special and peculiar focus. Flint arrow-heads and the old Stone Age are apt to look larger, more interesting and more important to them than Georgian town-halls or the twentieth century. They seem frequently to have perverted standards of value, preferring what is merely rare to what is beautiful.

It is the way of such people to extol and protect what is obsolete, past and dead at the expense of the present, the future and the living. Usually they live out their blinkered lives in houses and surroundings that would give convulsions to a first-year architectural student, quite innocently unaware that they are countenancing what should not be.

If it were not that the general public invariably insisted on considering local antiquaries as *ipso facto* authorities on architecture and amenity, and as general arbiters of taste, there would be no need to be thus uncivil about them. As it is, the public seems to need warning that antiquaries are very rarely reliable guides in these matters, and, to do them justice, seldom make any such claim.

The conferring of the title WITCH by popular acclaim brought nothing but reflected powers to the person so appointed, and her advice can seldom have proved very helpful to her credulous constituency. Hence the frequent witch-hunts and burnings by disillusioned clients.

For all our sakes let the hard-boiled archæologist stick to his specialised researches wherein he excels.

Assimilation

It is too much to hope, if it were indeed desirable, that every little building should be definitely a work of architecture. What is quite clear is that the generality of work-a-day rural buildings should be congruous with their setting, suitable to and harmonious with their surroundings, and ready and willing to be comfortably assimilated into the particular landscape of which they inevitably form a part. Many farms and country cottages are only seen at a distance by the general public, and in such cases it is *colour* that matters more than anything else—far more, for instance, than proportion or texture or any other architectural attribute.

It is really the roof that is all-important, and if that is more or less right, one can put up with a good deal of infelicity underneath it.

If the roof is to be of tiles, let them be rough-textured, preferably hand-made, which, besides being more durable than the smooth machine-mades, weather pleasantly and will soon tone acceptably with the neighbours, whether these be trees or older buildings.

If slates be used, let them be as soft-coloured as may be. The small rough greys that are readily obtainable give an effect that is infinitely better than that of the big smooth blue slates, though these in their turn are to be much preferred to their purple cousins.

If you must use asbestos (*must* you?), avoid the

livid pink sort as you would the scarlet fever, eschew even the more blood-like red, and cleave to russet brown or quaker grey. In the distance and in the appropriate districts neither of the two last need be more than slightly offensive. In Scotland or Cumberland or North Wales, for instance, though only a stone-built grey-slated cottage might be traditionally appropriate, one could scarcely grumble if a new bungalow had the elementary decency and good manners to cover the nakedness of its red-brick walls with plaster and whitewash, and its roof with grey asbestos. It would be in a rough sort of harmony with its setting, or rather with the traditional building associated in our minds with that particular sort of background. It would have no long-range offensiveness, it would broadcast nothing alien to its environment or violently shocking to our senses, as would the most impeccable south-country villa if built in such a situation. It would be a tolerably decent citizen and neighbour, and at a distance might even pass for a perfect gentleman.

What do defy and must defy for ever all attempts at harmonious assimilation into the landscape are houses dotted along a skyline, for their uncompromising angular shapes do not smoothly caress the sky like the tufted trees they perhaps replaced nor boldly stab it like chimney-stacks or steeples—they just interrupt what should be a smoothly flowing passage with their trivial, jerky little discord.

The sky is a very exacting and dangerous background, against which all but the architecturally distinguished and the most carefully outlined buildings will pose at their peril.

As to additions to congregations of buildings already existing, if these be sufficiently civilised to appreciate the courtesy one would take one's cue from them as a new-comer naturally should from old-established natives. Well-mannered new cottages, for instance, being added on to an old village would do their utmost to round off and complete the picture (probably a quiet and homely one) already composed by their predecessors. They would bear themselves discreetly and with great circumspection in the hope of proving welcome additions to the family, guaranteed and made acceptable by a general family likeness.

How often one may see new houses that are like swaggering strangers, knowing none of the family jokes or pass-words, that have insolently plunked themselves down on the edge of a cosy little gossip-party and been very properly left out in the cold. They have made no gesture of salutation, no concessions, no effort to make themselves agreeable or to respond to the architectural traditions of the place, and in return the old village just will not, cannot, " know " them.

The A.A. (Automobile Association)

THIS vast and wealthy association of motorists could, if it would, take a leading part in the preservation of amenities, both urban and rural.

Its thousands of members annually cover millions of miles for the sole purpose of enjoying the country, and it would not seem outside the proper scope of its activities if it were to show some helpful interest in rural preservation.

Meanwhile, it covers the land with useful signs in ugly lettering and unpleasing colours, erects tactless wayside telephone boxes at Stonehenge and other places where it should not, and yet (most properly) subscribes to the funds of the Council for the Preservation of Rural England.

It would seem indeed that the A.A. needs to determine its attitude to the amenities question, which would in turn enable many of us to determine ours to the Association.

Broadcasting

THE titanic, Martian-like masts of the sending and world-receiving stations are uncomfortable country neighbours on account of their too vast transcending of the human scale, but they are at present few and far between and have so far done little really dastardly in the way of overpowering or dwarfing the earlier works of God or man.

Any plea that general amenity might not be utterly disregarded in the siting of such stations would no doubt be ignored on some technical pretext that the layman would be incapable of refuting. There is no good technical reason, however, for squalid buildings, and the Marconi

Company in particular might have its attention profitably drawn to the admirable, imaginative and business-like architecture of certain wireless stations abroad, notably at Helsingfors and in Holland.

There is a secondary danger that at places like Chester (where the one idea of architectural propriety is to stumble along blunderingly in the ill-understood traditions of the past) the citizens would probably vote for a wireless station, an aerodrome or an electric power-house in sham "half-timbered Tudor."

One would think it self-evident that these strange and powerful new wines would demand and need new bottles—even strange and unprecedented bottles. At Stratford-on-Avon, which is a little tarred with the Chester brush, they are suddenly being modern enough and imaginative enough to provide a stout new bottle for a fine old wine in the building of the new Shakespeare Memorial Theatre. It would seem that Stratford has suddenly grown up and decided to put behind it its rather childish playing at "Ye Olde Oake Shoppe."

Besides the Sending Stations referred to, there are the innumerable little poles and aerials of the million offspring of these monstrous parents. Perhaps they are but a passing phase in the development of wireless and will soon be no more than a distressful memory; but whilst they are with us, might one plead that some little attention be paid to their placing and maintenance?

It is only the polychromatic intimacies of the family wash that endow the domestic clothes line with human interest, and as its big brother the aerial is denied these claims to our indulgence, it must usually be condemned for what it is, an untidy interruption of the view.

One can scarcely leave the subject of wireless broadcasting without reference to the great potentialities it possesses for the education of the people in those things that affect amenity. Cardiff has already realised its power and its responsibilities in this matter and set a notable example to the other Sending Stations.

Borough Engineers

BOROUGH engineers and surveyors are highly trained and highly qualified specialists, who have to wrestle with the many complicated technical problems falling within their province, such as of water supply, drainage, highways, structural safety and the like. As a general rule they discharge their duties with efficiency and devotion, and it is most unfair that odium should attach to them as a class for what is not their fault.

One cannot fairly expect an engineer or a surveyor to be also a competent architect (an ideal very seldom realised in fact),[1] but one might fairly expect him to refuse to have thrust upon him what

[1] Liverpool, Oxford, Shrewsbury and a handful of other towns are the happy exceptions.

are obviously architectural jobs for which he is as obviously incompetent.

In view of their almost universal ignorance of the principles of architectural design, one cannot imagine engineers and surveyors willingly undertaking jobs that are bound to show them up, and one can therefore only blame the councils for requiring them to do what is beyond the range of their knowledge and their training.

The one idea of the average engineer confronted with a job of work vaguely apprehended to be architectural is to slap on " ornamental features " in the shape of mere elaboration having nothing to do with the function or structure of what he is constructing. It is thus that the worst bandstands, tram-shelters, park gates, pavilions and public lavatories come into being, with their exuberant cast-iron arabesques and crestings and general dolled-up absurdity.

To do him justice, the engineer rarely designs these things himself, but orders from a manufacturer's catalogue what he considers " tasty " and what he thinks will be considered smart and classy by his council and the townspeople. It must be admitted that they generally accept what is chosen for them with perfect politeness, if not with marked enthusiasm.

Whilst this state of things persists and until we have learnt to employ architects to do our architectural designing, it is calamitous that so many of the manufacturers should still be working by the dimmed light of Prince Albert's Great Exhibition.

The current catalogue of a British manufacturer of "Ornamental Ironwork" is almost always a pathetic scrap-book of designs that were never anything but inept and vulgar, and that are now also thoroughly *démodé*. Where 1851 has been displaced it is to make way for 1901 *Art Nouveau*, the obscene contortions in that manner being still innocently accepted by the English years after they have been repudiated as an unfortunate *gaffe* by the rest of Europe.

Cast iron has only got a bad name in this country because for the last seventy-five years or so it has been consistently abused by being cast in ill-designed moulds. Much of Germany's modern commercial cast-iron work is unexceptionable, and that of Sweden is even better.

No material is more suitable for standardised mass production than is cast iron, and if only our manufacturers would scrap their old patterns and get really competent designers to supply them with new ones, the three words "Cast-Iron Railings" need no longer make one wince.

Bungalows

THERE is clearly nothing intrinsically vile about a one-storied dwelling, and, indeed, the most charming cottages celebrated in painting, poetry, history and song are definitely "lowly" in this quite literal sense.

No: hatred, ridicule and contempt do not attach to the bungalow merely because it is stairless (as though to a tailless fox), but because this perfectly reasonable type of building has been meanly exploited to its own degradation and the disfigurement of the country at large. For besides being the cheapest sort of human habitation (cheapest, that is, in first cost and if value-for-money is set aside), the reach-me-down, " carriage-paid-to-any-station " bungalow is also extremely adventurous.

That is putting it as politely as possible, for, in fact, the intrusive impertinence of the bungalow knows no bounds.

Before the War one had learnt to expect rows of villas to spring up along the lines of the public services—the roads and sewers, the water, gas and electric light mains—as do rank weeds along an open drain; but the bungalows are not thus regimented—they penetrate into the wildest country as lone adventurers or in guerilla bands. Many of them are what their purveyors call " semi-permanent," which means that dilapidations and patchings begin early, and that neglect will soon reduce their cocksure aggressiveness to a state of ruin.

Certainly one feels that with them it is light come, light go; and that they care no more for the country they are billeted on than barbarian invaders are wont to do.

But whilst they are with us they constitute England's most disfiguring disease, having, from sporadic beginnings, now become our premier epidemic. So few areas are still immune that it is unnecessary to give instances, though Peacehaven may still be cited as the classic example of the ravages of this distressing and almost universal complaint.

Manifestly there must and will be bungalows if there is a demand for them, and, as has already been admitted, the demand is often a very reasonable one, whether it be for a week-end or holiday camping-place or for a regular home. It is only with the anti-social placing of these little buildings and their gratuitously flashy or exotic appearance that fault is found. Laid out with sense and designed with sensibility, a seaside " Bungalow Town " might be charming.

The experiment needed to prove this assertion is a very simple one—but it has yet to be made.

Electric Power Distribution

WE are promised a complete grid of high-tension power transmission lines that shall cover these islands as with a net. We are also promised widespread industrial developments as a direct result, and of course proportionate prosperity.

That will be very nice.

But—and it is a very real question—what is this magic network going to cost us, not in money (that presumably is known and is of little general interest, anyway), but in amenity? What losses is this gain going to entail? All we know for certain is that they are going to be very heavy, inordinately heavier than they need be or have any right to be.

That we know from samples here and there all over the country, but particularly in North Wales. To judge by these first-fruits, the Electricity Bill governing these enterprises is drafted as are all such Bills, and makes no provision for the preservation of amenities. Alternatively, if there are any such provisions they are obviously quite futile.

The North Wales Power Scheme, for example, has expended much ingenuity and a great deal of money in contriving its little ancillary buildings in such a fashion as to be almost ideally out of harmony with their surroundings. In the foothills of Snowdonia, against a background of grey, tumbled rocks and wind-blown oaks, you will find cocksure little concrete " residences " for local power scheme officials, monstrously roofed with pale pink tiles, and that in the midst of quarries producing the best slates in the world—many of which quarries the Company actually supplies with power.

Could æsthetic impropriety go further ? The answer is, of course, " Yes—and it does," as witness the arbitrary harshness of the huge pipelines laid down the mountain sides with no attempt at decent camouflage by paint or planting or loose stone covering, and the transformer stations enclosed with saw-tooth corrugated sheets on which great ill-shaped letters spell out the undertaking's name.

If from examples in Norway and Sweden, Germany and Switzerland one did not know what hydro-electric power houses could be like—and *are* like in those fortunate countries—one might accept our mediocrities with a shrug as necessary evils. That, it seems, is all one can do about the transmission lines themselves, even when these traverse the loveliest little valleys of Merioneth, destroying their scale and importing a sense of sophistication and " Progress " of which they were till now so soothingly innocent.

Clearly the electrification of England will not be accomplished without severe shocks to amenity, unless we proceed better than we have begun.

Feng Shui [1]

" . . . China for a thousand years or more has been devoting its unrivalled artistic genius to this very question.[2] Unlike the Greeks, whose city policy still dominates Europe (except these islands), the Chinese have always looked to the countryside as their home. They accordingly definitely attempted so to harmonise human additions with natural features that a new and complex landscape might result, a fusion of conscious art with nature. This has been described as the science of ' adapting the residence of the

---

[1] *The Preservation of Rural England*, by P. Abercrombie (Hodder & Stoughton).

[2] That of the inevitable artificialisation of natural landscape.

living and the dead so as to co-operate and harmonise with the local currents of the cosmic breath.' The study is thus lifted on to a lofty plane; it is related on the one hand to the Chinese preoccupation with the fact that man is merely a temporarily detached and animated fragment of the earth, soon to return to it; and on the other to that intense veneration for natural scenery, and especially lofty mountains, which has caused Tibet, on the roof of the world, to be selected as the holy place.

" But besides this spiritual aspect there was the purely practical one: the people were too numerous to be penned in cities—they spread over the face of the country. The density of the population per square mile forced them to regard the country as equally subject to artificial treatment as the town. Unless it was controlled it would become a hopeless mess. Hence the practice and æsthetic of *Feng Shui*. The words *Feng Shui* actually mean wind-water, for it was considered (and justly) that the ultimate forms assumed by mountains and valleys were the outcome of the moulding influence of wind and water; but this notion has been immensely amplified so that ' at every place there are special topographical features (natural or artificial) which indicate or modify the universal spiritual breath.' Thus the alterations of natural forms by human intrusions have a good or bad effect according to the new forms produced. Infringements of these rules or neglect of their study are punished sometimes by Nature, at other times by man. Water, the archetype of humility, because it always seeks the lowest place, will resent interference with its natural bent, and as the humble can lose their tempers, it will rage forth from confinement, as happened so disastrously at Dolgarrog in North Wales. What would be the Chinese moralisation to be drawn from this? That in establishing the village at the bottom of the valley, and in the very pathway of the water, the projectors had given insufficient study to *Feng Shui*, or wind-water. If the village were already there when the original stream was a trickle, the confinement of the water into a lake by a dam higher up would have been found to alter the natural harmonies of the locality, and the village would have been moved out of harm's way. Human resentment in China is apt to be no less cataclysmic. Missionaries establishing themselves in some remote valley and building a neat corrugated iron tabernacle with spiked bell turret have been indignantly surprised when the population has arisen and massacred them—not by reason of any objection to their religious teaching, but because the pitch of the roof was, perhaps, too steep or the spike of their bell turret should have been domed or square-topped. Again, railway embankments and tunnels have been considered by the inhabitants to favour the circulation of a maleficent breath—a sort of whiff from the pit—and enterprising contractors have been astonished that their civilising efforts have met with furious opposition. The professor of *Feng Shui*, whose job it is to study and expound the shapes which the spiritual forces of Nature have produced and to prescribe the ways in which all buildings, roads, bridges, canals and railways must conform to them, is placed in a position of extreme power; and we ourselves can hardly hope to be able similarly to explode some flaring upstart bungalow or 'dark Satanic mill' or conflagrate the perpetuators of certain countryside-blasting advertisements in their own spirit.

"But whether we base our æsthetics upon Chinese premises or not, they have shown us in their exquisitely artificial country that it is possible to evolve a workable system.

"There must, it will be found, be no attempt to make new things imitate the old, or to aim at a bogus naturalism. That is where the eighteenth-century landscapists eventually failed; they were safe when dealing with vast stretches of country, adding a group of trees here, damming a lake there, enhancing and heightening the natural effects. But when they tried to introduce this naturalism into the gardens surrounding the house they merely produced wriggling paths and lopsided flower-beds in place of the older formal garden. So on our old roads the irregular trees and natural hedges are, where possible, to be kept; but new roads should be frankly treated as great regular avenues having a beauty of their own. Similarly, when dealing with old towns and villages their existing irregularities and picturesqueness must be respected; but if an entirely new community is to be planned for, then a frank formality is appropriate, tempered, of course, by any innate unevenness which the site may possess."

Gardens

EVERYONE is, or ought to be, grateful for wayside gardens (even the limousine motorist); and now that dust has been abolished and the number of passers-by has been enormously increased, the owner of a garden on the highway should feel it his duty as a good citizen to make as gay a show as he possibly can.

Here and there they do play up very gallantly—as in the Surrey village of Clandon, where a proper individual pride, aided no doubt by a vigorous local opinion, seems to ensure that each cottage garden shall every summer be a riot of flowers, not rare, but beautiful.

In some districts the soil is ungrateful to the gardener; in many more, smoke and industrial fumes affect the young plants even more adversely than they do young children. In these areas it is less disheartening to keep a nursery school than a nursery garden.

There are, however, wide stretches of the country where conditions are entirely favourable to gardening, which yet seem to breed no gardeners—much of Wales being in that category. In a land where fuschias, hydrangeas, azaleas and rhododendrons generally grow and luxuriate for the mere planting, and where daffodils " go wild," one would think that the idlest cottager would take the small amount of trouble involved in heeling-in a few plants, thereafter merely watching them grow. But in Wales a garden means a patch of potatoes and black-currant bushes, flowers being regarded as an amiable eccentricity, though perhaps a little worldly.

In certain parts the awarding of prizes for roadside gardens has mitigated this dour tradition, whilst on certain estates the free provision of shrubs and flowers to all who will plant and tend them has had a marked effect on the amenity of their immediate neighbourhood.

It is suggested that in every large garden—indeed in every garden that boasts a " paid hand "—a small part should be set aside as a reserve from which the owner could distribute suitable plants to his less fortunate neighbours. At no appreciable cost to anyone hundreds of seedlings, cuttings and surplus " dividings " could thus be made available for the general adornment of a whole parish, and there must surely be many garden owners who would rejoice to see flowers even outside their own preserves—probably many more than one might imagine from the little that is at present done about it.

Golf Courses

UNLIKE allotments, which from the point of view of beauty must be classed as necessary evils, golf links might well be called—by non-golfers—unnecessary adornments.

That they are adornments to almost any countryside is unquestionable, though the same can rarely be said for their club houses, which may be anything—gracious, fatuous or rankly poisonous. Golf courses are really specialised parks, often very beautiful parks, and as such they are most welcome, particularly in or near large towns.

In such situations, however, their lease of life is necessarily uncertain owing to the constantly rising value of the land for which speculative builders must always ultimately outbid the golfers; so that we are being perpetually faced with the paradox that where an open space is most urgently needed, both for health and amenity, there it is that the houses will most surely close in upon it and eventually swallow it up. That is, of course, whilst the land remains unrestricted private property, as does most of it at present, and it is (or ought to be) one of the chief objects of a town-planning or zoning scheme to schedule the pleasantest surviving patches of undeveloped country, especially if well-timbered grassland, as permanent open spaces.

This would mean the scheduling of many, perhaps most, of our suburban golf courses, in which case the owners would expect compensation from the Government, from the scheduling authority, or from the golfers. How far that expectation ought to be fulfilled is a large question outside the scope of this book, though one may remark that property adjoining a dedicated open space is almost invariably greatly enhanced by the security of amenity thus assured, and that large landowners might well find the value of their property as a whole increased by the sterilisation of a part; when no question of compensation ought to arise.

There are, however, few far-sighted enough to perform this operation themselves for their own sakes, still less in the interest of the public, which is why it is necessary to invoke official intervention. Even great corporations like the Ecclesiastical Commissioners cannot be trusted to administer their estates even with that enlightened self-interest which is as much as one dare ask of them.

At Highgate, for instance, the Commissioners own that beautiful stretch of open country on which is the golf course, and it was only through a fortunate accident that such pressure was able to be brought upon the Church as to force it to abandon its schemes for exploitation on commercial lines with the usual disregard for public amenity. As it is, only a respite has been obtained, and the ultimate fate of this precious lung is by no means certain.

The dedication of suburban golf courses as permanent open spaces does not imply the subvention of suburban golfers, and it is not a national movement for their defence and preservation that is being suggested. It is rather their playgrounds that are precious and of really national importance; it is these that we should seek to preserve, and not for the golfers only.

An average population through the daylight hours of the 365 days of the year of perhaps ·65 of a person per acre is not sufficient to justify their chartered immunity for all their usefulness as "lungs." They must show a better dividend in human enjoyment than that in return for their safeguarding, they must extend their field of usefulness quite a lot.

On Saturday and Sunday afternoons, for instance, they might open themselves to the general public of the district at purely nominal fees, the better-off and more leisured, as also the regular members, seeking more distant and select private courses if they find their home links too "popular." After all, most of them will have cars, and many of them will have been able to put in a round or two during the working week or on Saturday or Sunday morning.

Then there are the non-golfers and children— not to be utterly forgotten. Might not the course be free to them at certain stated times— perhaps on Friday afternoons and daily after sundown or six o'clock—whichever be the earlier?

No doubt the elderly hard-boiled devotee will feel that the end of the world is at hand. He may be quite right, but a shared manger should be better than no manger, and if he is too exclusive to tolerate official protection and regulation for his course, he may find himself left without a course at all.

Local Government

In the end the condition and appearance of rural England chiefly depends on local government administration, which in turn depends on the quality and zeal of the administrative officers.

During the nineteenth century and up to the present day there has evolved a complex system of local government, in accordance with which all the social and remediable legislation is delegated to Local Authorities. These services include Education, Public Health, Roads, Housing, Town Planning, Justice, etc., etc. The Local Authorities of the country spend about 250 million pounds a year on these services, partly out of rates and partly out of taxes. This sum is some five-sevenths of the whole of the pre-war revenue, and there is no system like it in Europe. On its proper working depends the whole welfare of local communities. Everybody, except perhaps cosmopolitan Cockneys, realises that it is the quality of *local* life in a nation that matters in the end.

A large number of intelligent people in the Universities, particularly Oxford and Cambridge, do not seem to have realised the existence of our system of local administration of social services; and the Universities are doing practically nothing to train men and women to take a useful part therein or to bring the enormous possibilities of this constructive work to their notice. They encourage them to go off to Kenya or as missionaries to China; or else the young men and women at Oxford and Cambridge think distilled æstheticism the most important thing, and spend their time writing unnecessary third-rate books or looking for swell jobs in London.

There are, for instance, splendid opportunities for those qualified as city and county architects. These are important key positions from the point of view of public works and of town planning. With an architect-artist in control in every town and county the face of England might be recharged with architectural significance. Do the Schools of Architecture and does the architectural profession take sufficient account of this? The only bodies that can get the right architectural tradition developed in local communities are, ultimately, the architectural profession and its schools.

As the organisation of the life of local communities can only be carried out through the instrumentality of local government and the immense corpus of delegated social legislation, the best chance for constructive civics lies in the local government service, and young men and women should be told this.

But in the Universities at present there are too many academics with the backward-looking bias, too much chilled meat afflicted by condescending Bloomsburian sniffing.

Oxford and Cambridge

So poignant is the contrast between these two University towns as they are and their civilised might-have-beens, that the author begs leave to quote from a recent address of his at the Cambridge Union rather than write afresh on so painful a subject.

"Then I came to Cambridge; and as an old Cambridge man I claim the privilege of being rude to my mother—my alma mater. . . .

"Having learnt Cambridge proper by heart, I found there was no way out of it at all. On every road ranks of grimacing villas headed one back and denied any scatheless escape even to such disfigured country as lay beyond. No one seemed to care; both dons and undergraduates were quite oblivious of this leprosy, and ever so normal and insensitive and jolly.

"So I gave it up, and at the end of a year escaped through the beleaguering belt of blue and yellow blockhouses in a reliable railway train. I have returned timidly to-day to find the siege intensified a hundredfold and that what were whips in my days are now scorpions indeed!

"For a non-industrial town Cambridge leads England in its peripheral devastation, and Oxford, if not actually runner-up, is but little behind. No two towns in England, saving the capital, have such noble architectural monuments to inspire them, or such an honourable architectural tradition; both are held to be centres not merely of learning and the humanities, but of civilisation generally.

"And this is the example of our elect—this! You may say, 'Ah, but it's nothing to do with the University, it's the Corporation, it's private property.'

"Then, in Heaven's name, *why* is it nothing to do with the University—how dare it merely look stupidly on and condone the outrage—has it no duties as well as privileges?

"If it is really blind, God help us all. If it sees but cannot bring itself to tackle a problem and a scandal at its own doors in some practical fashion, its pretensions to usefulness in our modern world are indeed excessive.

"And why are the sprawling suburbs and the even wider bungalow-belt private property, and chaotically and wastefully exploited for private gain regardless of amenity, order, dignity and even convenience, and cynically heedless of the commonweal?

"Had they cared to do so, the University and College authorities could themselves have bought up the country for miles around and preserved a gracious belt of green around their boundaries, and wisely and far-sightedly directed such growth and development as seemed necessary.

"Instead, they continued to own and generally to mismanage and neglect or recklessly exploit far-away landed estates all over the country.

"It is this failure, past and present, amongst the intelligentsia that makes me despair of the future. If this is Oxford and Cambridge, what can be hoped for Birmingham and Leeds?

" When this precious heritage—this lovely town with a heart of gold—this city of learning, this cradle of the arts and sciences, allows itself to be strangled and besmirched by land speculators and jerry-builders, can you wonder that I despair?

" Oxford and Cambridge, Cheltenham and Bath: Buxton, Brighton, Richmond and Bristol—what lovely places they might have been—how cynically have their chances been squandered and their charms been prostituted!

" It is no thanks to this generation or the last that they still remain less ungracious than Wigan and St. Helens, Hull, Sheffield and Swansea.

" Unlike St. Paul, most of us to-day are citizens of some *mean* city, and for those of us who know it, that means shame instead of pride—discomfort in place of pleasure. Perhaps there is a submerged subconscious shame and discomfort in most people, and it is for that reason that they refuse to face up to what is happening and see things as they really are; they are afraid—afraid of what they may find and what they may feel if they listen to Professor Abercrombie and myself—architectural agitators of the most dangerous and proselytising sort.

" If only we *were* dangerous—if only we *could* goad you to fury—fury with things as they are! If only we could make you love and hate as fiercely as we do—make you rejoice in beauty and wince at ugliness as at a blow!

" There would be hope if we could—but we can't. You are good, honest, practical, normal Englishmen!"

It is encouraging to be able to report that since the delivery of this jeremiad, the newly-constituted Oxford Preservation Trust has shown notable activity. Not only has it purchased considerable tracts of land about the city through the generosity of certain of its friends, but it is also taking an effective part in the guidance of the City Council through its Town Planning Committee.

A friendly coalition between the Council, the City Engineer and the Trust (whose members are drawn from all spheres) is beginning to bring about a general consensus in ideas about architecture and a united demand for care in design.

Cambridge also is awakening to its difficulties and responsibilities, and here the opportunity is to hand, as the Local Authorities have just decided to set up a joint Regional Planning Committee.

A Cambridge Preservation Society has been formed largely on the Oxford model, but with the aim not only of buying and holding land, but of influencing and focusing opinion in the University, town and county.

While the preservation or wise development of Cambridge and its immediate surroundings are to be the care of the Preservation Society, the rest of the county is being mapped out in a " Preservation Survey " by the Rural Community *the Octopus*

Council of the county, which has been active in the matter for the last two years. Through the Council's efforts Cambridgeshire is the first district to set up a panel of architects under the C.P.R.E. scheme, consisting of not less than three architects, with representatives also of Local Authorities and landowners. Founded primarily to give advice on the reconditioning of cottages under the Housing (Rural Workers) Act of 1926, this panel has already been approached for advice on other matters.

Paint

WHEN asked what he mixed his paints with to produce his astonishing effects, Whistler answered, " Brains ! "

To judge by results, one would guess that the British paint manufacturers' answer to the same question would be " Mud." The quality is superb ; it is the stock colours that are so lamentable.

If merely for protection, let us use the undoctored basic lead colour—the battleship grey of the Navy ; but if we go to all the trouble of having " fancy shades," presumably for delight, it seems a pity that so few of them should be in any way delightful.

Perhaps the manufacturers have exhausted their ingenuity in inventing the pretty names for their colours, which are certainly as engaging as those of a nurseryman's catalogue ; but it is a pity they cannot give a little of their attention to their actual pigments and put upon the market colours that are really gay and acceptable.

Our favourite colour is, of course, that strange and lugubrious plummy-purply-red that reminds one of dried blood. So unanimous are we in our preference that it might well be taken for our national colour, corresponding to the valiant orange paint of Ulster, which, on carts and barn doors, provides the only visible gaiety in that dolorous province. On many country estates no other paint but "dried blood" is used, even on the window sashes of the mansion-house itself. The effect is wonderfully dispiriting. In the matter of white paint we have no nicety or discretion: white is white, and that's that.

France and Sweden, particularly, know well that there are at least a dozen shades of "white," ranging from ash-grey to pale putty; and they use them with propriety and telling effect. Besides the "whites," blue and green are perhaps the most welcome out-of-doors colours; and it is exceedingly hard to find even tolerably acceptable shades of these ready-made. Most paint-makers will, however, try hard, if not always successfully, to match a pattern.

The way to get real brilliance is, of course, to apply your finishing coat of colour over a dead white under-coating.

Seeing that the appearance of most buildings is so greatly affected by the colour of their exterior wood and iron work, no apology is offered for this digression.

It is a commonplace that many squalid-looking little houses built of mean or unpleasant coloured materials can be transformed out of all knowing at a trifling cost by colour-washing. The whites, pinks and yellows have for ages been universal favourites for this purpose, and look well in almost any setting, especially in combination. If lime-wash be used as the basis, colouring matter can be added *au choix*, and the cost of beauty-doctoring by this means is trifling.

Some years ago the author submitted a collection of whitewash recipes to the Department of Scientific and Industrial Research for testing and report. The experiments and tests then made placed the following at the head of the list for durability and protective qualities:

> "Place 1 bushel good fresh lime in a barrel with 20 lbs. beef tallow; slake with hot water and cover with sackcloth to keep in steam. When the lime is slaked, the tallow will have disappeared, having formed a chemical compound with the lime. Dry colours may be added to produce any tint desired."

Parkways

THERE are those who profess to deplore the unsightliness of our new trunk roads and switches, but their dissatisfaction, if analysed, would probably be found to derive not from the roads themselves but from their boundaries.

There is surely something rather noble about the broad white concrete ribbons laid in sweeping curves and easy gradients across the country—something satisfying in their clean-planed cuttings and embankments.

But in the buildings that quickly crop up on either hand there is nothing at all noble or satisfying. Whether bungalows or garages, tea-shops or villas, their nastiness is assured. It is this uneconomic "ribbon development" along the main roads that is so rapidly destroying such country amenity as is still left near our growing towns; and we are doing little or nothing to combat it.

The disfiguring little buildings grow up and multiply like nettles along a drain, like lice upon a tape-worm: we may be rude about them like that—but we do nothing to check their increase.

We do not even make them contribute to the vast cost of the fine new road that has attracted them: we make them a present of it and all its amenity, and of the site value it has created, when surely they should be heavily penalised for their spoil-sport impertinence in daring to exhibit their deformities in a public place.

Are we not a little mad?

In certain parts of America they manage things very differently, the new roads being bordered on each side not by uniform ten- or twenty-foot bands of mere "spare room," but by irregular patches of the original country with its old hedges and trees, grass, orchards, brooks and what-not—all included within the scheme and State freehold of the road, and with it constituting what they call a " Parkway."

This pleasant name is in no way illusory (a refreshing thing in itself), for on such roads one certainly feels that one is traversing a drive threading a far-flung natural park, which is indeed the case. The fact that the said park may be twenty miles long and nowhere more than a few hundred yards in width is neither here nor there, save as testimony to the ingenuity and economy of its planner.

In England, if a new road happens to traverse a five-acre meadow diagonally, we acquire a strip of the uniform standard width across it—jealously fencing in our acquisition with uncompromising concrete posts and wires at great expense and leaving the two surplus corners of the field as relatively useless, cock-eyed little remnants for the original owner or farmer to use as best he may. Cases may often be seen where the new fence belonging to the road is separated from the original field hedge by no more than a few feet, leaving a ridiculous and quite useless wedge of " dead " land between them. The road alteration between High Wycombe and Oxford are commended for study in this connection.

In the Parkway system it is customary to acquire the whole of each field, wood or other enclosure that the new road will traverse, making their original fences the boundaries of the road. Discretion is, of course, exercised and the boundary may be extended or withdrawn as the assured and permanent amenity of the road may seem to demand. Where the skyline is quite near to the highway, an effort would be made to secure it, and such eminences would probably be planted with suitable deciduous trees to enhance their height and general effectiveness.

A meandering footpath generally accompanies the road in a *dégagé* sort of way—much as an enterprising child will attach itself to a sedately walking grown-up—and when a stream has to be crossed, it will usually have a pleasant little footbridge all to itself, perhaps with the water banked back into a pool or little waterfall beneath it, as far removed from the noisy traffic bridge as conveniently may be.

Where the road dives into a ten-acre wood—it might be into the outpost of an illimitable forest for all one knows—no fences are apparent and glades have been cleared inviting one to wander into its shadowy interior, perhaps with a picnic basket from the car that stands parked in a little siding well clear of the passing traffic.

Where the full-width road would entail the destruction of particularly fine old trees or be out of scale with its surroundings, the Parkway planners have a pleasant habit of dividing the road into two half widths, one for up and one for down traffic, with a narrow island between, perhaps of original woodland, so that a journey out and back is here and there acceptably diversified.

Thus bought in its " natural " units of complete fields, it appears that the cost of acquiring the extra land over and above the minimum strip is a mere trifle, certainly as compared with the total cost of the whole roadway; the cost of new and special fencing along the road is saved; and what amounts to a great new public park is secured as a by-product just where it will be most appreciated and used.

The great and signal merit of the Parkway system, however, is not so much this open-handed giving of beauty and amenity to the new roads, but the blessed thrusting back of ugliness to a discreet and relatively harmless distance.

Leaving New York by way of the Bronx one immediately enters upon a Parkway that carries one into the heart of Westchester County along a green belt of grass and trees, which, because of its unfenced friendliness, is far more greenly welcoming than most completely rural and honest-to-God country. As a fact, of course, the land on either hand is thickly populated, and to turn off the Parkway by any one of the frequent switch roads is probably to find oneself in a pleasant dormitory village, a place of open lawns and shady avenues, where most of the little houses are sightly enough.

After the bricky babel of New York, however, one would not exchange the trees of the Parkway for the most unexceptional buildings, and one is grateful for their discreet withdrawal.

How far more urgent is the need in England

for pushing back our so much less seemly buildings to a little distance, where possible behind a screen of trees, must be clear to all who use our new trunk roads.

Let the doubter halt on the new short cut between Hanwell and Uxbridge, or leave London by the new Great West Road from Kew. Then let him go to Henley and note how wonderfully the undistinguished little houses along the road to Oxford conceal and dissemble their presence behind the trees of the fine old avenue.

But by the time this is printed the avenue may have been destroyed.

Petrol Pump

THESE ubiquitous engines have gained an undeservedly bad name as eyesores for three bad reasons. They are subconsciously associated with the slatternly array of variegated advertisements that commonly deface filling stations; the stations themselves are too often placed where their presence is an impertinence, and the actual pumps—usually a mixed bouquet of violent reds, yellows and greens—are so painted not to produce an acceptable harmony, but the most reverberating discord.

There is no denying that one cannot pass a wayside filling station without having one's attention distracted to it by its bludgeoning importunity; but having noted and resented its presence, one just passes.

Yet there is nothing repulsive about the pumps themselves. They may not be consummate examples of functional designing, but they are reasonable and seemly machines enough, and where ranged neatly along a grass plat and painted some acceptable and uniform colour are by no means unsightly.

In these days of spare tins and reserve tanks there is no possible excuse for the wayside petrol pedlar; and the way to discourage him is to refuse him your patronage.

Throughout twenty-five years of motoring the author has sedulously avoided any dealings whatever with such destroyers of highway amenity—invariably filling at some station (when possible a decently discreet one) within the actual boundaries of a town or village, not certainly at the clamorously touting pumps that attempt the motorist's seduction at every main road entrance to such places. Often there are two rival establishments glaring at each other across the road, selling identical wares at the same controlled prices. The result is a doubling of ugliness and presumably a halving of the profits to either one of them, which does not seem a very sensible arrangement.

Spirits in the liquor sense cannot be sold except by those holding a licence, which can only be obtained on the payment of fees after good cause has been shown for its granting and a public demand has been proved.

Is there any good reason why the retailing of

motor spirit should not be similarly limited before the country is so overburdened with a plethora of pumps that petrol-selling ceases to be remunerative, resulting in the disfiguring of our highways by derelict stations even more unsightly in their dilapidated abandonment than in their flaunting youth?

Railings

WE are a nation of railers-off and railers-in—the Englishman's home is his cage. Why? Are we so much more savage and predatory than the Americans, in whose country, park or garden railings are almost unknown and where private lawns lie trustfully open to the road without provoking trespass or outrage? At most they will have an elegant row of white posts with chains slung between—more as a frill and a finish than as a serious deterrent to anything but wheeled vehicles.

Yet the flower-beds bloom unravished, the turf is not dishonoured with litter, nor are the fruit trees robbed or mutilated.

The Continent, too, seems to get along very well without our elaborate defences, confidently lining hundreds of miles of its unfenced public highways with productive fruit trees. Even the inhabitants of the Balkans, whom we are prone to regard as less civilised than ourselves, substitute good manners that are gracious for palisades which are not.

During the late War Mr. Churchill had a plan

for melting down all the railings round our parks and square gardens, and converting them into munitions, but the Armistice supervened. This Chinaman's-Roast-Pig expedient for the revealing of our urban greenery having proved abortive, might we not yet deliberately uproot these disfiguring barriers—or do we in truth love them for their own sake and for all that they stand for and symbolise?

No doubt we should be told, " Oh, but you have no idea how destructive the Public would be—especially on dark nights."

Very well, if we have no idea, by all means let us form one—but on adequate evidence. Let the railings of one half of the gardens in Eaton Square be removed by way of a test case, and let us see the result and have an authoritative report on the desperate experiment.

One can scarcely believe that the atrocities thus risked would be so very frightful.

And why, in a country where spring-guns and man-traps have been long since made illegal, are *spiked* railings still permitted? They are even placed waist high on bridges and around flower-beds where everything else invites the leisurely to lean and linger. With care and practice one *can* contrive to lean on spiked railings such as those that so surprisingly enclose the Hudson Memorial Bird Sanctuary in Hyde Park—but it is an uneasy business.

They are more of a provocation than a deterrent to a healthy-minded boy, who risks death or mutilation each time that he accepts their hostile challenge.

It is strange that we should so cheerfully risk the immolation of our children by disembowelling spikes such as no humane person would dream of placing round his dog kennel.

The barbed wire that now enmeshes so large a part of Salisbury Plain, and what was until lately free and open downland, has, one must believe, some economic justification, but is none the less deplorable.

Railways

IN their youthful exuberance and adolescent years of growth, as also in their prosperous maturity, the British railways did many things of which in their rather harassed old age they are no doubt properly ashamed.

They habitually used their monopolistic powers with a ruthless disregard for general amenity, though, to be sure, there are many early railway stations that reveal a genuine if misguided desire on the part of their designers to harmonise them with the building traditions of their respective localities. Shrewsbury station, sprawling below the old castle, tried *very* hard, and is quite pathetically baronial. That desire, however, did not persist for long, and we got the more or less standardised railway-station architecture with which we are all so painfully familiar.

There is little to be said against an intelligently flexible standardisation if the archetypal model be a good one—indeed, everything to be said *for* it in the case of a railway, especially from its own point of view. The point at issue is that the current railway building tradition is absurd, inefficient and obsolete, and long overdue for revision.

The "New" architecture of the Continent, after the manner of Corbusier, with its uncompromising insistence on function and its unadorned austerity, would surely better become a railway station than anything in Engineer's Renaissance or Teashop Tudor.

As such stations fall due for reconstruction, is it too much to hope that they will rise again transfigured into something more reasonable? Likewise, could not station yards and approaches in general be rendered less squalidly repellent?

A little care in the marshalling and maintenance of advertisements, a little tree-planting and a little paint are often all that are needed to redeem such places and turn them from their present forbidding dreariness into something almost welcoming.

One of the most gracious and satisfying *ensembles* in the world is the terminal railroad station at Washington, where, from the soft-lit *foyer*, one steps out into a leafy piazza whence tree-lined avenues radiate to the chief traffic centres of that lovely city. There are no advertisements but much extremely distinguished sculpture.

Immense sums are spent both by the railway companies and the places they serve on advertising their sometimes recondite attractions. If all that money were devoted actually to making themselves a little less unlike their flattering posters, a railway tour of England might soon be undertaken with greatly diminished anguish—perhaps ultimately with pleasure.

As our unprotected roads become hemmed in by the buildings that sprawl on either hand they are rapidly losing their old attraction. The railways are at least free from this reproach, and mostly traverse the very heart of rural England.

In their new bid for popularity there is at any rate one slogan they might adopt with perfect fairness: " To see the real country—travel by Train."

Soldiers

The Army and the Air Force (and to a lesser degree the Navy) are like the blow-flies—where they settle, there you will find corruption and all unpleasantness.

Soldiers, like sailors, don't care.

Peace and beauty dissolve away at their uncreating touch, their buildings insolently challenge and howl down whatever of quiet loveliness may lie within their range.

The ancient villages scattered along the Wiltshire Avon that borders Salisbury Plain—the very Plain itself—they are what the military have made them, with their mutton-fisted barracks, their depressing married quarters and desolating hutments. Surrey, too, has suffered many things because of them.

We talk pleasantly enough about disarmament;

and meanwhile the Army and the Air Force build and build, not pleasantly at all, but to the grim designs of Royal Engineers. As architects, Royal engineers are even more deplorable than the common sorts, and how should they not be? In their proper sphere they are magnificent; at constructing roads, drainage and water-works, temporary bridges, and fortifications; at mines, too, and saps, trenches and latrines they may well be supreme.

It is at demolition, however, that they really excel—they are the architects of destruction.

But architectural designing—no. They would probably retort, " We are not allowed to waste public money on frills." But who—having once seen them (there are examples)—wants the " frills " of a Royal Engineer? They are not the sort of thing that the delicately minded would choose to dwell upon.

A barrack block in competent hands can be made to yield an impressive, even beautiful effect without a penny-worth of ornament by sheer virtuosity and a proper mastery over materials, mass and line; as scores, probably hundreds, of continental barrack buildings do.

Let the would-be barrack designer study the great Pensions Building at Acton and the modern American High Schools, or try to wrest the secret of Wren's triumphant success from the simple stateliness of Chelsea Hospital. From that urbane and noble building let him turn about to face the enormous vacuity of Chelsea Barracks—

lately added to in the same style of Peabody-Pauperesque.

Then let him think hard—along the lines suggested in Chapter VIII. If there were any sincerity in our talk of disarmament, should we continue to dot the country with great warlike establishments built of brick and concrete—apparently for all time.—without a thought for their convenient conversion to peace purposes in the near or distant future?

If, pending their substantial diminution or abolition, the fighting services could henceforth arrange to house themselves and the implements of their trade in decently planned settlements, sensibly placed and laid out with a view to the needs of an enlightened civil occupation in days to come, one might be a little less eager to dispense with their fabulously costly services. Even to be able to point to two or three pleasant little (potential) villages completed each year in return for our hundreds of millions would be better than nothing at all.

Standardisation

THE tiresome person who can use his eyes to some extent, but not his head, is apt to be shocked, on principle, at all proposals for standardisation, without considering specific cases on their merits. It is the sort of person who damns good materials out of hand merely because they are often misused and made fools of by incompetents.

Because manufacturers and contractors habitually employ cast iron, concrete, plate-glass, pitch-pine, varnish, glazed tiles, and moulded brick-work in an improper manner, he will say and even believe that all these things are æsthetically bad in themselves, which is manifest bosh.

In the same way, because nearly all builders' ironmongery, and ready-made doors and lamp-posts and tramway standards are ill-designed, he will confidently assert that "Standardisation means ugliness."

The Americans are more logical and realise that, given a really good original, the more it is multiplied (within wide limits) the better.

The mass production of our old five-shilling piece made its spirited St. George not one whit the less admirable, whilst even the Britannia that still rules the British penny so competently continues to give us a quieter satisfaction. The fact is that St. George and Britannia (like all good designing) defy that sort of familiarity that breeds contempt.

For a few or for many dollars (it matters little which) the American manufacturer commissions the best artist or expert he can find to make him designs and models for what he intends to turn out—whether it is a door-knob or a window. Then he starts "production" by thousands or by tens of thousands, so that the happy American architect is able to specify and build-in cheap stock-pattern fittings that are nearly always excellent in design and workmanship and sometimes real works of art.

Of course America still has its banalities, but they are no longer the general rule as in England—despite the patient mission work of our Design and Industries Association.[1]

The charming new telephone call-boxes in London, designed by Sir Giles Gilbert Scott, R.A., the finely lettered street-name tablets of the Borough of Kensington, and the well-proportioned steel casements manufactured by Hope's, Crittall's and the other big firms: all these things have been standardised, and they are all good. They could indeed scarcely have been bettered; but it is not a long list. It might, no doubt, be added to, but not without some reflection.

We English have a snobbish belief that "Cheap and Nasty" represents cause and effect, and we have done our best to substantiate the heresy by only making good things in such small quantities that they are too expensive for general use and remain the luxuries of the exacting rich. Though this is true of the crafts and applied arts, our engineering and more utilitarian industries are imaginative and progressive enough, whence the Morris motor-car and the tenpenny half-penny vacuum flask.

Trees

THOSE who care for amenity are generally on the side of the trees—so easily destroyed, so hard to replace.

---

[1] The "D.I.A.," 6 Queen Square, W.C. 1.

But not always. The wrong sort of trees in the wrong place are almost invariably what they are and where they are through the will of man, and they can be almost as disharmonious and intrusive as his more impudent buildings.

From a landscape point of view at least, God is an excellent forester and makes very few mistakes.

It is only through man's impertinence and misguided assiduity that the rarer and horrider sorts of fancy conifer, the variegated laurel and holly, the monkey-puzzle and the such-like stock-in-trade of the suburban nurseryman are now a plague in the land. Their only merit is that they usually embower those Desirable Residences which would be really too indecent without an evergreen screen of some sort, though their exotic presence in the Park-like Grounds with which estate agents delight to credit the more pretentious villas, lacks even such excuse. Their usual effect is merely to spoil and vulgarise a good honest meadow.

On the other hand, the transformation that wise tree-planting can work in an otherwise undistinguished street or along an uneventful and possibly dull stretch of road must be seen to be believed. A conducted tour of France, Germany and America for our County Councillors is clearly indicated, but they might in the meantime at least send delegates to see Cheltenham, Welwyn, the Hampstead Garden Suburb, and the approaches to Dorking and Dorchester.

The planting of an avenue is the most gracious work to which a good citizen can turn his hand.

Water

WHETHER in crinkled movement or reflective repose, there is something in water uniquely attractive to the average man. If only as a place to lean and spit from, there is no place so popular as the village bridge.

Unfortunately, however, a superstitious urge seems to impel the semi-civilised to cast their discarded goods and utensils into the nearest available water, whether this be a crystal chalk stream, a horse-pond or a mill-race. Old bicycle wheels, jam pots, tins, bottles, cast-off clothing, kettles and broken chambers are the common objects usually to be noted in such waters where they adjoin the humbler sort of houses.

This unfortunate habit seems a difficult one to break, and if there is no one with sufficient authority over the dishonoured water or over those who so defile it to make an effective fuss, a large pit provided conveniently near might serve to convert the slatterns to the decent burial of their rubbish.

No really ambitious park or garden is held to be complete without water in the shape of a pool, a long canal or a fountain, often contrived with difficulty and at great cost; but where we find water already provided by the bounty of Nature we seem to have little gratitude for it, certainly small respect.

The great majority of our towns and numberless villages owe their very foundation to the presence of a river; yet how many of these seek ungratefully to hide their ancient origin and to dissemble their good fortune by covering over their running water with roads and buildings, leaving it to sneak through them unobserved in culverts and between the indifferent backs of their least considered houses.

The Backs at Cambridge are a perfect example of due honour being paid to a parent river, with the result that this half-mile of the Cam is famous the world over, and justly. The town of Evesham has by no means forgotten its river, and has acknowledged its indebtedness by courteously contriving a pleasant little park upon its banks.

Shrewsbury, too, shows a proper pride in being " On Severn," though it is a beautiful little village on that same river some ten miles below Gloucester that is perhaps the most engagingly water-conscious place in England. It is called Newnham.

Epistola Epilogica

CLOUGH! YOUR BOOK IS NOT AN EASY ONE TO epilogise. You don't exactly offer a back inviting a gentle pat from the Hon. Sec. of the Council for the Preservation of Rural England. We have, indeed, been disputants: at Cambridge we, simple children, attacked each other before the assemblage of wise youth—yours the pessimist motion—"Gone was Rural England beyond Redemption"—mine the piddling optimist reply —"There's hope for the old Dog yet." But there was a paradox in these rôles—your pessimism was so lively that it lugged you up from a bed of fever (if England had been so far gone was it worth while recovering oneself?);—you appeared fiery-eyed, check-trousered (think of it, within the Victorian Gothic of the decorous Union!) to shout, as did the gay Mademoiselle de Limueil, when she lay a-dying,

"Tout est frelore, bigoth,"

with full emphasis on the Gothic oath; whereas

Epilogica

my optimism was so gloomy that my geological hopes looked to another Ice Age to purify the Countryside, having recently seen some golden sand emerging with the unimpaired glory of the Triassic formation from near our Liverpool University, whose Waterhouse buildings and Workhouse surroundings surpass even your lurid descriptions. If "All is lost, by G–d!" or a lapse of time comparable to a geological epoch is necessary to clear up the mess, why do *You* write a Book and build Portmerion on a peninsula of North Wales or do *I* race about the country, endangering my matrimonial stability, to rouse up people to take Action *now* ?

Seriously, is not the damage largely skin deep ? I believe ten years would convert the derelict desert between Birmingham & Wolverhampton into an incipient Jungle; and will many of what you rightly call Blasphemous Bungalows, blaspheme as long ?

And is not much of England still virgin country, *intacta* ? Last week within forty miles of London we landed from a voyage by boat up a certain river, which shall not be named; we journeyed on land ten miles or so through fields & villages unblasted & unblaspheming, at last along field tracks, through field gates, past a group of thatched (some newly done) cottages to a grey Georgian house which looked out one way on the line of B. . . . Downs, the other to the ridge of the C. . . .: quiet country, modest views, insufficient to draw the sightseer to whom I give no further indication of its whereabouts. But the owner has a fear: immediately around him he is safe; but what if a gasometer should appear on the line of Downs or a jerky row of houses on the Ridge? There is no security, for has not the like indignity been offered to Windsor? He seriously contemplates buying up that Ridge ten or twelve miles away to protect his view. It is not his view only that would thereby be preserved, but that of everyone who raises his eyes to these hills, either living there or motoring towards London. I hope he will do it, but should it be necessary, should it depend upon the hazard of one man's purse? So no place is really safe.

I leave you to tell us how to restore as swiftly as possible what is decayed, to show us how new growth (as you yourself demonstrate practically at Portmeirion) can add to the beauty of landscape, and to advise what country should be kept free from human additions. For these your Devil's Dictionary, which is also an Angels' Enchiridion, gives admirable constructive advice tempered by lusty curses. But I would like to add, though not to daunt your zeal, a list of those offenders, conscious or not (the last probably most dangerous), whom we have to convert.

First the *Government*, whose heads, we know, are with us, but whose tails are allowed to wag at times disastrously: you have handled the Soldiers, who have more excuse than most people for dis-

Epilogica

regarding the feelings of others; but was it necessary to lease the Wye Valley to a foreign firm of stone-quarriers?; was it wise to hand on the New Forest to the Forestry Commission, which is forced to pursue an economic policy, when there are thousands of acres of dull derelict agricultural land that would be enhanced by tree-planting?; should not the reference to the Electricity Commissioner have envisaged the effect of lattice standards striding over Dover's Hill & past the town of Chipping Campden and over the Welsh Mountains?

Next the *Local Authorities*: their sins are generally those of omission. They have failed to take advantage of the Town Planning Act and apply it, as it can be applied, for Rural purposes. Comparatively few of them (outside the big Towns, whose problem is a suburban one) grasp in any way the powers for Rural Preservation which the word " amenity " in the Act implies. How frequently when an ingenuous questioner asks, "Can't you stop this?", the reply is—" No, we have no powers "—" under the bye-laws " being murmured *sotto voce*, as a sort of " over the left." The questioner then writes to the paper demanding new Legislation: the powers are there all the time! At length, it is true, some use is being made of Advertisement control: and the Government's Petrol Pump Bill, if it is retro-active, may do much; but there are heavier things than advertisements to remove.

Next the *General Public* that flies to the country,

to motor in, to week-end in or to reside in for good. Does not each one consider his own use of it and forget that there are others building on the road-front to escape a few pounds for a new road (the local authorities here step in with an exorbitant road specification); choosing a spot that gives him a good view but spoils that of others; using whatever materials come easiest to hand, irrespective of surroundings?

Can we add *Landowners* as a clan to our list of offenders? The Farmer-owner who wishes to recoup his recent-years' loss by the selling of road frontages for houses can barely be blamed. But big landowners have done the same, often through apathy, because it is the easiest way to satisfy a demand for houses, though they would have ultimately benefited themselves and the people who were to live in them if they had laid out little building schemes at right angles to the main roads.

The *Multiple Shops* are among the worst offenders, though fortunately they rarely thrust themselves into the open country. But they make up for it by upsetting the harmony of many a village and country town. Their brutal stock fronts botched on to older buildings, cutting half-way through the first-floor windows, bring a shout of town vulgarity that drowns the quiet charm of the place.

You have dealt with *Surveyors* without a knowledge of architecture who design houses; but are

Architects themselves always without offence? What about those who would refuse to meddle with such unremunerative stuff as small houses unless they are done by the dozen, or who testify against any form of standardisation as inartistic, or any kind of Control as dangerous to artistic originality?

The *Manufacturers* of Standard Houses and Stock Parts—windows, doors, etc.—have offended continuously: a little co-operation between them and architects might produce modest little houses, like those of the late eighteenth and early nineteenth century.

But the other, general *Manufacturers* who plump for a country site, are a more difficult proposition: they must satisfy the demands of Shareholders on the one hand and of the manual workers on the other. In fact, the whole country is up against you here except Mr. Churchill, who wants to keep the Factories in the towns for some obscure fiscal reason, and a handful of people like you and me, who have no investments and who live on our wits. But we don't want to keep the Factories out of the country (except in certain places), so long as they will behave decently; the worst feature of the Paper-mill on Sanford Lock near Oxford is the chimney, and the worst feature of the chimney is the bulbous top which the manufacturer thought was a concession to beauty.

Indeed, we agree—don't we?—that most of

these offences are the result of Ignorance rather than Malice: pure Diabolism, as I think you say somewhere, is not really common. But this multiplicity of offenders, the number of æsthetic Baptisms required before the country can enter upon a state of Grace, makes the job of regeneration no slight one. So we decided to form a Council as various as possible, and even drawn from the same elements that produce the offenders! Our nucleus, of course, was a little group of unabashed enthusiasts—the SCAPA that has long been carping at advertisements and first sought to look after the country generally; the Commons and Footpaths; the Society for the Protection of Ancient Buildings and the Ancient Monument Society, godchildren of our President, Lord Crawford; the Garden City People; the R.I.B.A., whose then President, Guy Dauber, made this his major labour; the Town Planning Institute; the National Housing and Town Planning Council, and the Royal Society of Arts. But what could a rabble of enthusiasts and technicians have done but shout shrilly and draw pretty pictures? Enter then the solid weight of the Local Authorities, County, Urban and Rural Councils Associations. Next, equally weighty, the possessors of England's soil, represented by the Central Landowners and the Country Gentleman's Association, backed by their advisers, the Surveyors' Institution and the Land Agents & Estate Agents. Through the Institute of Builders we hope to get at those who

Epilogica

build in the country. Then the users of the country, *in ambulando*, according to their various grades of speed: the walkers, the bicyclists, the motorists (we've forgotten the flyers!). But we haven't forgotten the real country people, those who quietly live there: we get them through the Rural Community Councils and the Women's Institutes. These latter, of course, provide us with our keenest workers and—may I add?—sharpest critics. Last to be mentioned, but among the first to join us, your "Country Executor," The National Trust. Throughout the Minister of Health has countenanced us and his Ministry (per G. L. P.) has guided our footsteps.

From these wide sources is our C.P.R.E. drawn; and when we sit round a table there is unanimity that the country should be preserved and decently developed: though there are, maybe, differences of opinion as to how this should be done. But if Ribbon Building and other enormities are ever to be scotched, this is the hand to do it, reinforced as it is by the legal skill of Sir Leslie Scott, by the inventive genius of Sir Richard Paget, by the Press, who have backed us from the start, and directed by our devoted secretary, H. G. Griffin.

And now those shy folk, the Publishers, seem to have spotted us: Geoffrey Bles is producing this book of yours. From his motto he seems to be a star-gazer, but you have brought him down to Mother Earth: may She reward him bounteously at your hands. And so I won't give him any more stuff to set up in type. But if our Council should institute an Order of the Daisy Chain, I would propose *You*, Clough, for a Knight Grand Cross; it would become you well.

Yours ever,
Patrick Abercrombie.

How we treat "Places of Historic Interest and Natural Beauty."

Stonehenge.

[*The label* Café *has been applied in error to the wrong building. It belongs to that on the extreme right.*]

Hendon : Welsh Harp Lake.

Two Blatant Intrusions.

See Section on Electric Power Development in "Devil's Dictionary."

What Christchurch thinks of Christchurch Priory.

Refined and Well-proportioned Bank at Shrewsbury (recently built).

CONTRAST IN SHOP-FRONTS AND GROUPING.

New Buildings on the Bath Road.

Farnham, Surrey.

Two more Blatant Intrusions.

(See p. 127.)

An Old Whitewashed Cottage in North Wales and—

A Costly New Bungalow in the Same Neighbourhood—no Vulgarity spared.

CONTRASTS IN "ASSIMILATION."

A Skyline Bungalow in Wales and—

An Easier Problem less successfully solved in Warwickshire.

Contrasting Treatment of Roadside Tea-rooms.

England is Cheap To-day!

Motor Service Station—Usual Type.

Successful Treatment of Motor Service Station on the Kingston By-pass. Contrast with Previous Illustration.

[Reproduced by permission of the Controller, H.M. Stationery Office.

Pleasant and Suitable Post Office at Evesham. Designed by H.M. Office of Works. (See p. 122.)

Two Views of Broadway, Worcestershire.

CONTRAST IN ROADSIDE DEVELOPMENT.

Oxford.   "Build-as-you-please."

Near Marlborough.   A Disciplined Group.

IN THE VALE OF LLANGALLEN.

The view and—

What looks at it.

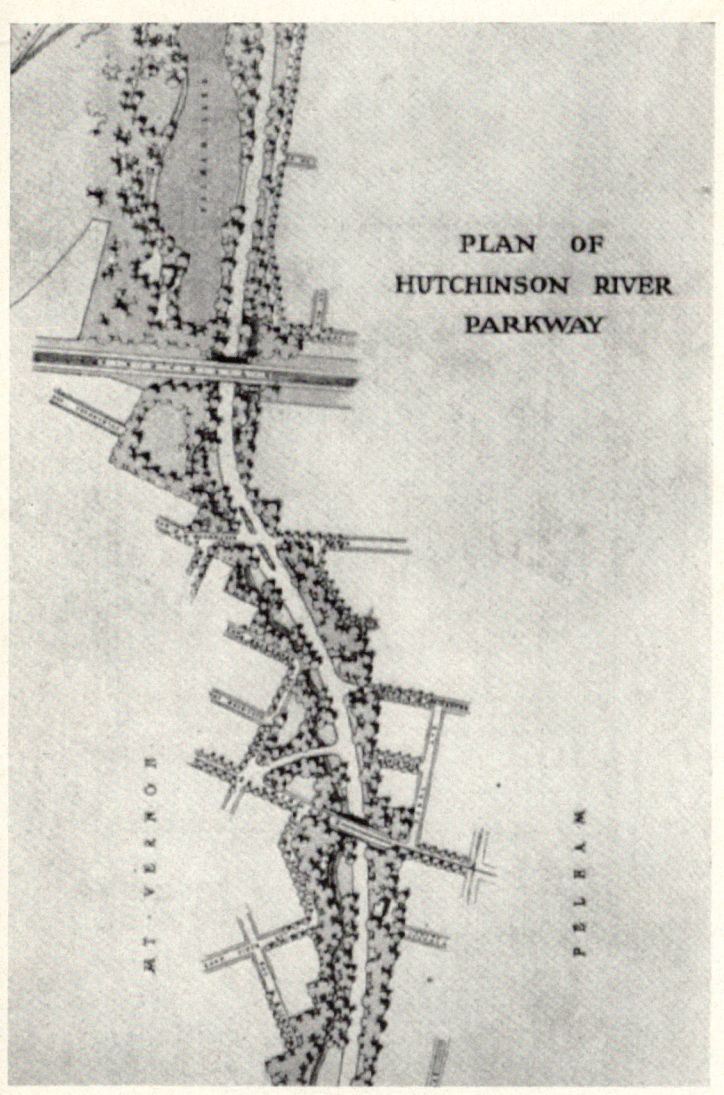

See Section of "Devil's Dictionary" on Parkways.

The "COTTABUNGA"

(Regd.)

THIS CHARMING BUNGALOW COTTAGE delivered, carriage paid, to any goods station in England or Wales, ready to erect, for - - - **£245 : 10 nett.**

"COTTABUNGA" buildings may be seen dotted all over the Countryside, North—South—East—West, and are giving universal satisfaction. No better value at the price is possible, and if you would enjoy the comforts and luxury of this artistic residence this coming summer place your order NOW.

Our illustrated Catalogue, No. 103, containing full particulars and a full range of other Bungalows, Pavilions, Motor Houses, Chalets, etc., post free to any address.

BROWNE & LILLY, LTD.
THAMES SIDE, READING

Telegrams: Portable, Reading.   *'Phone: Reading 587*

[Reproduced by permission.